APHRA BEHN

Mrs Aphra Behn

APHRA BEHN
THE INCOMPARABLE ASTREA

BY

V. SACKVILLE-WEST

NEW YORK / RUSSELL & RUSSELL

The frontispiece portrait
drawn by J. GOWER PARKS
from contemporary sources

PR
3317
.Z5
S3

FIRST PUBLISHED IN 1927
REISSUED, 1970, BY RUSSELL & RUSSELL
A DIVISION OF ATHENEUM PUBLISHERS, INC.
BY ARRANGEMENT WITH THE EXECUTORS OF
THE HON. V. SACKVILLE-WEST
L. C. CATALOG CARD NO: 75-102540
PRINTED IN THE UNITED STATES OF AMERICA

The stage how loosely does *Astrea* tread,
Who fairly puts all characters to bed.

POPE

FOREWORD

THE FOLLOWING STUDY of Aphra Behn does not pretend to be either detailed or exhaustive. All the available material has already been collected by the Rev Montague Summers into his *Memoir of Mrs Behn*, prefixed to his edition of her works, and I have therefore thought it unnecessary to crowd a very slight sketch with every scrap of information or reference. On the other hand, if I have gone at some length into the destructive arguments advanced by Dr Bernbaum, it is because Father Summers in his Memoir has allotted only a brief footnote to Dr Bernbaum's two pamphlets, and also because I have had the advantage of studying several articles in a Dutch magazine, which have appeared since Father Summers' Memoir was written.

My warmest thanks are due to Father Summers for his kindness in answering various enquiries and for the loan of books; and also to Sir Edmund Gosse who, with his accustomed generosity, placed not only his rare editions of Mrs Behn, but also his time and erudition at my disposal, and who was good enough to express his willingness to read my proof-sheets, with which, but for his recent illness, I should unhesitatingly have troubled him.

V. S.-W.

APHRA BEHN
(1640–1689)

I

APHRA BEHN, that good-humoured lady, that lady
' dressed in the loose robe de chambre, with her neck and
breasts bare; how much fire in her eye! what a passionate
expression in her motions! how much assurance in her
features!' was born at Wye near Canterbury in the summer
of 1640, and disappears at an early age from the shores of
England and the pages of reputable biography. From the
moment when she was carried, an infant in arms, past the
hop gardens and into the church under the green hill at
Wye, she set out on a career rich in contradiction and controversy. Her parentage, the place of her birth, the status
of her father, the spelling of her name, the scenes of her
childhood and adolescence, the spelling of her husband's
name, the very existence of her husband, all have been sub-
jects of dispute. It makes matters ticklish and exciting for
her biographer. Is he to call her Aphra, Ayfara, Aphara,
Aphora, Afra, Apharra, Afara, or, more fantastically, Aphaw
or even Fyhare? Is he to call her Amis or Johnson? Is
he to write Behn, Bhen, or Behen? Is he to keep her at
Wye or to send her off to Surinam? If he is to send her to
Surinam, is he to send her there once, or twice? Is he to
believe in Van der Albert and Van Bruin? She lies under
a black marble slab in Westminster Abbey, and cannot
answer these questions.

But let us say straight away that Aphra Behn is no Shake-

speare, the smallest clue to the detail of whose life would
be precious and worth pursuing. The biographer picking
his way through the tangle of dates and facts, pouncing
with delight on some unexpected corroboration, shredding,
destroying, and discarding finally some plausible theory, un-
ravelling with patience as one unravels a muddle of string
and rolls it up again into a presentable ball,—the biographer
may be tempted into examinations too minute to be anything
but wearisome to the general reader. It is enough if he can
persuade his reader to take his store of specific knowledge
for granted, and allow him to proceed to a broader picture,
the picture of Mrs Behn in her loose robe de chambre, a
little slovenly perhaps, and often a little too coarse, but
always generous and warm and kindly, writing away at her
slap-dash dialogue in her sordid London room, interrupted
by young Grub Street knocking at her door in the confidence
that they will be met with jokes and sympathy and common-
sense, and, if need be, with the help of a not too well-furnished
purse. There was a time when the name of Aphra Behn
might scarcely be mentioned, or mentioned only apolo-
getically; it was synonymous for all that was bawdy both in
life and literature. ' She was a mere harlot,' says one writer
crossly and primly, ' who danced through uncleanness.' But
although she might lay her scenes in brothels and bedrooms,
although her language is not to be recommended to the
queasy, and although in her private life she followed the
dictates of inclination rather than of conventional morality,
Aphra Behn, in the history of English letters, is something
much more important than a mere harlot. The fact that
she wrote is much more important than the quality of what
she wrote. The importance of Aphra Behn is that she was
the first woman in England to earn her living by her pen.

True, the matchless Orinda had preceded the incomparable Astrea; but Orinda was not a professional writer; she
had not her living to earn; she was neither a novelist nor
a playwright; she was only a prosperous amateur dabbling

in poetry, the apostle of friendship, the hostess of a literary salon. There had been the Duchess of Newcastle, but the Duchess of Newcastle was a great if eccentric lady, who, though she wrote, and wrote frantically, for fame, could in no sense of the word be called a competitor in the jostling world of literary jealousies. Mrs Behn, on the other hand, entered the open lists. She was an inhabitant of Grub Street with the best of them; she claimed equal rights with the men; she was a phenomenon never before seen, and, when seen, furiously resented. The anger of her critics and rivals was equalled only by her own anger at not being dispassionately judged. Well aware of her own position as a pioneer, and confident in her own powers to carry through the task she had undertaken, her tongue and her pen grew tart under the injustice of organised attacks. ' A woeful play, God damn him, for it was a woman's.' But although sometimes angry, and often hurt, she was never discouraged. Novels, translations, poems, plays streamed from her quill, together with vituperations and retaliations fired at her detractors. From the moment that she took to writing, to the day of her death, she was never worsted; by her stubbornness she rendered a service to her sex, and it was no small service. A troop of women followed in the steps she had so painfully cut; Elizabeth Rowe, Mary Pix, Eliza Haywood, Jane Barker, Penelope Aubin, Mary de la Rivière Manley, to name but a few, were her direct successors. Her works may not be read, but it is as a pioneer that she should, to her eternal honour, be remembered.

2

IT WAS ORIGINALLY supposed, and most writers have perpetuated the error, that her father was a barber named John Johnson of Canterbury; an examination of the parish register of Wye reveals the truth: that there is no mention either of Johnson or of his having been a barber, but that on the 10th of July 1640 Peter and Ayfara, the son and daughter of John and Amy Amis, were baptised together at the church of SS Gregory and Martin. The entry is not difficult to decipher, and reads:

Peter ye son
                & of John and Amy Amis. July ye 10th.
Ayfara ye daughter

Yet even here, coming down to modern days, the spirit of inaccuracy and mystification which attended Aphra Behn throughout all records of her life was still at work. It was apparently impossible for the Vicar of Wye, in 1884, to read the entry standing in plain English before his eyes. Sir Edmund Gosse having come into possession of a manuscript book belonging to Anne Countess of Winchelsea, and having read therein a note to the effect that Mrs Behn was born at Wye, wrote to the Vicar for any confirmation that might be found in the annals of the parish. Was there, he asked, any record of John Johnson or his daughter? The Vicar searched his register, and replied—Yes, Ayfara, daughter of John and Amy Johnson, was baptised on July 10th 1640. Now, it would be impossible, even for an unlettered person, to read the name Johnson into that entry. It has moreover been stated that the 'Quality, Trade, and Profession' column has been left blank; now, there is no such thing as a quality, trade, and profession column in the register. It is, indeed, a very curious curse that has been laid upon the legend of Aphra Behn.

The entry at all events helps to put an end to the fable about the barber, for which Anne Countess of Winchelsea in that manuscript note was alone responsible, and establishes the fact that Aphra's maiden name was not Johnson but Amis. Ensuing difficulties are not so easily disposed of. In the first place, the sources of information are extremely unreliable. We have to place our faith in Aphra's own words, which are too frequently the words of the born novelist rather than of the seeker after truth; and in the

account of her earliest biographer, some of whose statements
are, to say the least of it, improbable. Aphra was a precocious child, early engaged in writing verses, and her health,
like that of many precocious children, gave her parents cause
for anxiety. I suggest that the fact of her having been
baptized on the same day as her brother Peter points to the
probability that they were twins,[1] a probability strengthened
by the delicacy of the girl. She herself tells us that she was
' but sickly, and very apt to fall into fits of dangerous illness
upon any extraordinary melancholy '; in other words, what
we should call a nervous child, and one whose imagination
was the more liable to be stimulated by the remarkable
scenes and events she was presently to witness. According
to the usually accepted story, the Amis family, of Wye, left
England for Surinam, now Dutch Guiana, where John
Amis had been appointed ' Lieutenant-general of six-and-
thirty islands, besides the continent of Surinam,' an honour
designed for him by his relative, Lord Willoughby of Parham.
So far so good, and had John Amis lived to enter upon his
duties several vexed questions would surely be settled for us
by official correspondence and other records. But the yeoman of Wye was never destined to reach that distant country
of Caribs and savannahs. ' My father died at sea,' says his
daughter briefly. For Mrs Amy Amis and her children,
however, there was no turning back; the ship bore them
inevitably onward, till after the wastes of ocean they sighted,
even as Columbus and Raleigh had sighted, the coast of
South America, and landed more or less as castaways there
where they had hoped to arrive as rulers. It must have been
a change from Wye.

They were received, it appears, if we are to trust Aphra,
with honour, for although they ' did not intend to stay upon
the place,' they were presented with the best house in the
country, called St John's Hill, which ' stood on a vast rock

---

[1] Not necessarily, however, as children were often ' saved up ' until two or
three could be baptised together.

of white marble, at the foot of which the river ran a vast
depth down, and not to be descended on that side; the little
waves still dashing and washing the foot of this rock, made
the softest murmurs and purlings in the world.' After this,
the account becomes a little vague. In spite of not intending
to stay upon the place, Aphra seems to have settled down to
enjoy the amenities of Surinam;—and here the inevitable
discrepancy becomes apparent, for although her biographer
says she went there as a child, Aphra writes of herself as a
grown-up person, sharing the life of adults.

For the moment, though, let it pass. The Amis family
is in Surinam, six thousand miles from Wye; ' 'Tis there
eternal spring, always the months of April, May, and June;
the shades are perpetual, the trees bearing at once all degrees
of leaves and fruit, from blooming buds to ripe autumn;
groves of oranges, lemons, citrons, figs, nutmegs, and noble
aromatics, continually bearing their fragrancies; the trees
appearing all like nosegays, adorned with flowers of different
kinds; some are all white, some purple, some scarlet, some
blue, some yellow; bearing at the same time ripe fruit, and
blooming young, or producing every day new.' They grew
familiar with the fields of cassava; with the spectacle of
macaws, parrots, and canaries flashing above the wild water-
lilies in the lagoons and trenches; with the note of the twa-
twa, like a silver gong; they listened to the kiskadee saying
' qu'est ce que dit? qu'est ce que dit? '; they knew Gran Gado,
the grand God, and his wife Maria, and his son Jesi Kist;
they met Indians of strange aspect, coming down from the
mountains carrying bags of gold dust. Besides all this there
were many other marvels; the Amis family threw logs of
cedar on their fire; lit their rooms with candles of aromatic
substance, that cast its perfume all about; dined off the flesh
of the armadillo, a little beast that was like nothing so much
as a rhinoceros, all in white armour, so well jointed that it
moved as though it had nothing on; and went on many
expeditions, whether to search for young tigers in their

dens or to teach the Indians to kiss, but all equally delightful,
and all equally different from anything they might have hoped
to find in the neighbourhood of Canterbury.   Aphra had
her hair cut short; she had a taffety cap with black feathers
in it; her brother wore a stuff suit, with silver loops and
buttons, and an abundance of green ribbon, so that when
they went about with Mr Trefry of Cornwall, who was so
good a mathematician, and could speak both French and
Spanish, and Harry Martin, and played on the flute to the
Indians, they dazzled those poor naked savages so much
that there was no end to their admiration.

But it was not only with Mr Trefry and Harry Martin
that Aphra and her brother went about.   They were accom-
panied by a far more important person, who, although jet-
black in colour and occupying an inferior position, being in
fact no more than Trefry's slave, was of royal birth; and
by his strength, pride, and beauty distinguished in Aphra's
eyes above all other men.   She knew him as Cæsar, his
slave-name, and to him she was his Great Mistress; but
Trefry had had the truth of his story from him, nor was it
long before Aphra had it also.   This Cæsar, who had been
sold into slavery by the treachery of his grandfather and
jealous rival, the King of Coromantien, was no less a person
than Oroonoko, prince of that country, now fretting in
captivity (for ' he had a spirit all rough and fierce, that could
not be tamed to lazy rest '), and torn moreover from the
arms of his beloved Imoinda, whom he believed to be now
dead after being dishonoured by the embraces of his grandfather.   Here was a story to enlist the sympathies of honest
Trefry, ' who was naturally amorous, and delighted to talk
of love as well as any body.'   Oroonoko thought himself
extremely fortunate to have fallen into the hands of so
kindly a master, and Trefry for his part was well pleased
with a discernment that had penetrated the reserve of his
royal slave; by the time they had finished their journey up
the river the two were friends rather than slave and master,

and Trefry had promised that at the first opportunity he
would restore Oroonoko to his own country. In his turn
Trefry recounted to Oroonoko the tale of the most charming
Black that ever was beheld on their plantation, herself all
ice and unconcern, though no man of any nation ever beheld
her that did not fall in love with her. ' I confess,' said
Trefry (he is sitting with Oroonoko and several English
gentlemen at a feast prepared by Oroonoko's fellow slaves
in his honour), ' I confess, when I have, against her will,
entertained her with love so long as to be transported with
my passion even above decency, I have been ready to make
use of those advantages of strength and force Nature had
given me, but oh! she disarms me with that modesty and
weeping, so tender and so moving, that I retire, and thank
my stars she overcame me.' The company laughed at his
civility to a slave, but Oroonoko applauded the nobleness
of his passion and nature.

You see, of course, what is coming. The charming
Black is no other than Imoinda, who has likewise been sold
into slavery, and Trefry, leaving the lovers in each other's
arms, runs down to Parham House to find Aphra and bring
her to enjoy with him the spectacle of their reunion. Aphra,
already on the best of terms with Oroonoko, was very ready
to befriend Imoinda. The pair were ' scarce an hour in a
day from my lodgings '; they ate with her, and she entertained them with stories of nuns and the lives of the Romans.
So the time passed pleasantly enough for Aphra in the company of her two black friends, though, try as she might, she
never could convert Oroonoko to the Christian idea of the
Trinity.

3

I T W A S I N *Oroonoko, or, The Royal Slave*, that Mrs
Behn was later to set forth these her experiences in Dutch
Guiana. Oroonoko is the direct ancestor of the ' noble
savage,' the stripling that

> . . . sportive, gay, and bold,
> And with his dancing crest
> So beautiful, through savage lands
> Had roamed about, with vagrant bands
> Of Indians in the West.
>
> The wind, the tempest roaring high,
> The tumult of a tropic sky,
> Might well be dangerous food
> For him, a youth to whom was given
> So much of earth, so much of heaven,
> And such impetuous blood.

Mrs Behn, indeed, spares no pains to make her hero as attractive as possible. She is never tired of alluding to the greatness of his look, the haughtiness of his air, the awefulness of his eye, the nobility of his soul; he could run, wrestle, and pitch the bar; he could chase snakes and tigers; his royalty shone through his humble suit of Osenbrigs; nor was his physical prowess his only virtue, but his wit (a quality much esteemed by Mrs Behn) and discourse were admirable, and in her opinion he was capable of reigning as well and governing as wisely as any prince civilised in the most refined schools of humanity and learning.

Add to this that he was ' as capable of love as it was possible for a brave and gallant man to be ' and her enthusiasm for her hero becomes the more understandable, for she never made any bones about her conviction that love was the pleasantest thing in the world.

She wrote *Oroonoko* many years later, after she herself had passed through the vicissitudes of love and fortune and had grown definitely into her character of the loose-living, kindly, successful Astrea of Restoration London. She wrote it, however, not in her hey-day; not when she frequented Wills' Coffee-house with Dryden and Otway and Mr Creech; not when her plays were running at the

Duke's Theatre and the angry critics were yelping at her
success; but as a sick woman approaching the end of her
life, and reviving, even as she wept with pain, the memory
of that country where all things by nature were rare,
delightful, and wonderful. Past memories of youth revived
too, and the contrast came over her, so that unnecessary
phrases slipped into the narrative, about the passing of youth,
for ' certainly, nothing is more afflicting to a decayed beauty,
than to behold in itself declining charms, that were once
adored ; and to find those caresses paid to new beauties, to
which once she laid claim; to hear them whisper, as she
passes by, That once was a delicate woman '.

The story was extremely popular. It was frequently
reprinted; it enjoyed a ' superior edition on a fine wove
paper, hot-pressed '; it was included in collections of
stories; it was translated into French and German; it
provided Southerne with the material for his tragedy;
Garrick and Mrs Cibber appeared at Drury Lane as Oroonoko and Imoinda in yet another version. It was a new
departure in fiction, even if we reject the theory that it
was ' the first novel of emancipation.' Reject it I think
we certainly must, in the absence of all internal evidence
to prove that Mrs Behn, despite her proper indignation at
any definite ill-treatment of the natives, held views upon
the abolition of slavery. She probably took it quite as a
matter of course that black people should exist in subjection
to white; she was not preaching; she was telling a story.
And telling it extremely well. *Oroonoko* goes with a vigour,
an energy, a picturesqueness, which make it readable to-day;
and towards the tragical end, when she comes to the death
of Oroonoko and Imoinda, and to ' the parting, the eternal
leave-taking of two such lovers, so greatly born, so sensible,
so beautiful, so young, and so fond,' she writes with a vivid-
ness that is really moving. That it should be so is no small
triumph. What could be further from us than the scene of
her tragedy, an obscure little colony in the seventeenth

century? or than the loves of two natives of Coromatien? or more unfamiliar than the spectacle of a negro tearing out his own bowels? Yet, by the direct and hardy blows of her pen she does contrive to infuse some quality that is stirring and tremendous into a relation so remote and so improbable.

4

BUT NOW COMES Dr Bernbaum, and says that none of this is true. Mrs Behn, he says, never went to Surinam at all. She never saw a marble palace floating on the English Channel, therefore she never saw Surinam. Her father, he says, was not her father, nor was he ever appointed Governor of Surinam or any other colony. She never knew Oroonoko; never came within measurable distance of him. If she could lie about Prince Tarquin, she could lie about Oroonoko. Was his name, indeed, Oroonoko? Was she not thinking of the winding river called Orinoco, whose Indian significance is ' coiled serpent'? Was her own name, indeed, Mrs Behn? Was there ever a Mr Behn? What proof have we of his existence? Gildon says there was a Mr Behn, but then Gildon was a liar. Poor Aphra, there is not much left of her.

Dr Bernbaum's arguments come under two headings. The first argument goes to prove that Mrs Behn had never been in Surinam; the second argument, which grows naturally out of the first, goes to prove that the *Life and Memoirs* was full of false biographical detail, and moreover was not written by one ' of the fair sex ' but by Gildon himself. Let us examine these two contentions in their order.

Mrs Behn had not been to Surinam. There was no reason why she should have been there. Her father was a barber, and why should a barber be appointed lieutenant-governor of six-and-thirty islands, besides the continent of Surinam? Why, indeed? but it is unfortunate for

Dr Bernbaum's argument that subsequent discoveries should have proved that her father was not a barber, and that his name was not even what Dr Bernbaum, in common with everybody else, believed it to be. True, this discovery had not been made at the time when Dr Bernbaum wrote his pamphlet, but it is significant that he should have overlooked the inconvenient remark in the *Life and Memoirs* that Aphra was ' a gentlewoman by birth, of a good family,' related to Lord Willoughby, governor of Barbadoes and half-owner with Lord Carlisle of Surinam. Dr Bernbaum's original premise thus nullified, we must fall back upon the rest of his evidence. Of this he advances plenty, relying half upon what we may call internal evidence, i.e. Mrs Behn's descriptions of Surinam, and half upon chronology. The internal evidence theory appears to me childish and negligible, the chronology more worthy of consideration.

Dr Bernbaum's principal grievance against Mrs Behn is that her descriptions of Surinam tally too well with the descriptions given by George Warren in his *Impartial description of Surinam*, published in 1667. Warren omits to mention the palms and orchids; so does she. He omits the cayman; so does she. He describes the electric eel; so does she. He says the armadillo smells; so does she. He does not say that the girl babies among the Caribs have a band tied round the calf of their leg; nor does she. At first sight, the case seems to be going strongly against Mrs Behn, but soon Dr Bernbaum grows too eager, and our caution is aroused. He enquires sarcastically, for instance, how ' the practice [of kissing, which, she alleges, she taught to the Indians] could have been so enjoyable to the Caribs, whose lips are pierced with holes, in which are inserted thorns or pins '; but he refrains from quoting the following words from *Oroonoko*, '. . . needles, which they used only as tools to drill holes in their ears, noses, and lips, where they hang a great many little things, as long beads, bits of tin, brass or silver beat thin, and any shining trinket.' Mrs

Behn, then, knew perfectly well that the Caribs thus orna-
mented their faces, and Dr Bernbaum's implication of her
ignorance at once collapses. His own words might well be
turned against him, ' whatever did not please her fancy she
at will suppressed or modified.'

Of course, in the foregoing passage I have picked only a
few examples from the mass of detail which Dr Bernbaum
produces. The curious may be referred to his pamphlet
and allowed to judge for themselves. It is an ingenious piece
of work, but from the point of view of internal evidence it
entirely fails to convince me. I can see no reason why she
should not have refreshed her memory with Warren's little
book. She was a young woman when she left Surinam, she
was a woman of nearly fifty when she wrote *Oroonoko*,—
and she says that she wrote it in a few hours, and ' never
rested her pen a moment for thought.' We have, besides,
Gildon's remark, ' I saw her myself write *Oroonoko* and keep
her turn in discoursing with several then present in the room.'
Mrs Behn's claim that she wrote it in a few hours may be
(and certainly is) exaggeration; Gildon's remark may, of
course, be untrue, though to my mind it bears the stamp of
truth as not being a thing that anybody would invent; but
in any case there is nothing improbable in the suggestion
that Mrs Behn scribbled with Warren open at her elbow.

The chronology is much more puzzling, and there are
several extra points of discrepancy which Dr Bernbaum,
for all his ingenuity, seems to have missed. I have chosen
to relegate to an appendix the details of this examination,
which however absorbing to the student can present little
more than a problem in arithmetic to the general reader.
The date at which she went to Surinam, how long she
remained there, and the date at which she returned are of
very little interest beside the cardinal question of whether
she ever went there at all. And that she did go there I am,
in spite of Dr Bernbaum, firmly convinced. Sir Edmund
Gosse, indeed, goes so far as to suggest that she went there

twice, once as a child and once in later life, but although this would cover the facts and might also explain the confusion which resulted in the mind of her biographer (for Mrs Behn was dead in 1696 when the *Life and Memoirs* appeared, and consequently was not able to correct these errors), there is absolutely no written evidence to confirm his theory. We are nowhere given any hint that Mrs Behn twice undertook the long, difficult, and perilous journey to Surinam. On the other hand, there is a great deal of evidence that she did, at some period of her life, go there. There is the fact that not one of her friends, relatives, or contemporaries ever contradicted her statement. It was never called in question. Yet as *Oroonoko* was not published till 1688, at least twenty-three years after her presumed return from that sojourn, either her contemporaries were particularly gullible to accept suddenly and without surprise an account of travels which they had never before, in a period of over twenty years, heard her mention; or else—which is not credible—for over twenty years she had been laying her train and preparing their minds for the reception of *Oroonoko*. There is the fact that in the dedication of *The Young King*, produced in 1679, that is, nine years before the publication of *Oroonoko*, she refers quite casually to the ' three thousand leagues of ocean she [her muse] has measured, visited many and distant shores,' so that she ' feared the reproach of being an American, whose country rarely produces beauties of this kind . . . this youthful sally of my pen, this first essay of my infant poetry.' There is the small circumstance that Gildon says of *The Younger Brother* that Mrs Behn took an incident of her plot from ' a true story of the brother of Colonel Henry Martin, and a lady that must be nameless,'—Colonel Henry Martin being that Harry Martin whom she knew in Surinam. These are details, doubtless, but they all help to swell the evidence.

Finally, a fact conveniently ignored by Dr Bernbaum in this place, though mentioned by him in a footnote else-

where, there is Southerne's remark in the dedicatory epistle
to his tragedy of *Oroonoko:* ' I remember what I have heard
from a friend of hers, that she always told his (Oroonoko's)
story more feelingly than she writ it.' She had, then,
talked, and talked often, about her travels. So it is fair to
assume that her travels were a matter of fact and not of
fancy.

5

I T H I N K, therefore, that we must accept the commonly-
credited story that Mrs Behn wrote from personal knowledge
of Surinam. Whether there were any such people as
Oroonoko and Imoinda is another question. Dr Bernbaum
does not suggest what I am about to suggest; it may seem
strange that so obvious a compromise should not have
occurred to him, but it must be remembered that he was
concentrating on one point and one only; to discredit
all the accepted versions of Mrs Behn's early career. My
compromise,—a very mild one,—is that Mrs Behn, having
been to Surinam and seeing in Surinam a useful background
for a story, invented, or at any rate amplified, the figures of
Oroonoko and Imoinda. She founded, I think, her fiction
upon stories which she had been told. Let it be remembered
that she had in her the elements of a true novelist, and
Trefry or another may well have told her of the loves of
slaves, which her romantic imagination would instantly have
magnified into the loves of slaves royally born; or some
rebellious slave of ' noble mien ' may well have taken her
fancy; a thousand combinations are possible. The story of
Oroonoko and Imoinda as it stands does not, to my mind,
quite carry conviction. There is Trefry's account of their
reunion, which I have already quoted; this smacks too much
of the coincidence of fiction. There is the account of
Trefry sitting at dinner with his slave, an imprudent and
improbable neglect of hierarchy on a plantation, even if you
make allowance for the friendship and the private under-

standing which Mrs Behn says existed between the slave
and the master.   Appearances would have to be respected,
whatever Trefry's private feelings might have been.   There
are the accounts of Oroonoko's feats of heroism and endur-
ance; of his continuing to smoke while his ears, his nose,
his private members, and one of his arms were hacked off;
all seen through the magnifying-glass of romance.   That
Oroonoko existed in some prototype I do not doubt.   That
the story stirred Mrs Behn, always alive, temperamentally,
to the heroic and the romantic, and educated up to it by her
reading of La Calprenède and Mlle de Scudéry, I do not
doubt either, else how should we account for Southerne's
comment?   But that she was relating actual occurrences,
as an eye-witness, in conscientious reproduction, I would
not for one moment maintain.

Furthermore,—and this is a point not made by Dr
Bernbaum—some introductory sentences in both *Oroonoko*
and *The Fair Jilt* bear a suspicious resemblance to one
another.   Let it be borne in mind that *The Fair Jilt* pur-
ports to be a true history; Aphra lays particular stress on this
in her dedication: ' This little history . . . has but this
merit to recommend it, that it is Truth; Truth, which
you so much admire. . . . For however it may be imagined
that poetry (my talent) has so greatly the ascendant over me,
that all I write must pass as fiction, I now desire to have it
understood that this is reality, and matter of fact, and acted
in this our latter age, and that in the person of Tarquin I
bring a prince to kiss your hands, who owned himself and
was received as the last of the race of the Roman kings, whom
I have often seen, and you have often heard of.'   She could
scarcely have said it with more insistence.   Yet it is obvious
that Prince Tarquin (' I shall give my fair jilt a feigned
name, but my hero must retain his own '), had he in truth
been a historical personage, would be easy to identify.
Certainly Aphra could lie, and lie with conviction, when it
suited her purpose.

Now let us compare the parallel sentences:

Oroonoko	*The Fair Jilt*
I do not pretend, in giving you the history of this royal slave, to entertain my reader with a feigned story . . . nor in relating the truth, design to adorn it with any accidents . . . I was myself an eye-witness to a great part of what you will find here set down; and what I could not be witness of I received from the mouth of the chief actor in this history . . .	I do not pretend to entertain you here with a feigned story, or anything pieced together with romantic accidents, but every circumstance to a tittle is truth. To a great part of the main I myself was an eye-witness, and what I did not see, I was confirmed of by actors in the intrigue, holy men, of the Order of St Francis.

The words are almost identical. It is clear, too, that Mrs Behn was quite prepared to reinforce her statements by the use of circumstantial detail, even to the extent of compromising the Church: ' What I did not see, I was confirmed of by actors in the intrigue, holy men, of the Order of St Francis.' Not ' holy men ' merely; not vague holy men; she was very thorough: even the order to which they belonged is specified. It is the luxury of the novelist.

The analogy between the two stories is, in another way, suggestive. What is true of *The Fair Jilt*, is that its author had lived in Antwerp,—that is beyond dispute,—and used Antwerp as the background for her tale of an imaginary hero. Is it not reasonable to suggest that what is true of *The Fair Jilt* is also true of *Oroonoko*, that its author had lived in Surinam, but invented the hero? That she used Surinam, in fact, in the same manner as she used Antwerp? It seems to me that this may well be the solution. There is also the coincidence that *Oroonoko* and *The Fair Jilt* were written in the same year. It is a pity, of course, to come to this conclusion, for if we were to accept the theory that

Mrs Behn had never been to Surinam, the fact would emerge
that she was a far finer novelist than has hitherto been
supposed. She would leap at once in our estimation from
the respectable class of the realist to the giddier heights of
the imaginative writer. If it were indeed true that Warren's
little book was the only mine from which she cut her jewels
of description,—if hearsay were indeed the only incentive to
her splendid indignation,—then we should cease to regard
Oroonoko as a partial photograph and should look upon it as
an entire creation. Mrs Behn might have been a liar, but
she would have had in her the genuine stuff of the artist. As
she borrowed the plots of her plays, so would she have
borrowed the tropical scenery of her story, and left it an
intenser thing than she had found it. As it is, we must be
content with the hope that Oroonoko and Imoinda, glisten-
ing, ebony, tortured figures that they are, running with
little rivulets of blood, crowned with their martyrdom, bear
little resemblance to life on the plantations, even in the
seventeenth century, but rise as splendid evocations complete
in themselves, from the odds and ends of legend that drifted
about the verandahs of Surinam. This in itself, though for
different reasons than those which have usually been adduced,
would entitle *Oroonoko* to be considered as the masterpiece
of Aphra Behn.

I

THE SECOND PART of Dr Bernbaum's argument is concerned with the authenticity and reliability of the *Life and Memoirs*, and that resolves itself into the problem of Charles Gildon. Gildon was a literary hack, who had his living to earn, and was not above accepting any job that came his way; but he was evidently also one of those irritating and curious, though not uncommon, characters, like Psalmanazar and Ireland, who delight in literary mystification for its own sake. He rejoiced in pretending to 'secret intelligence'; in the use of misleading initials; in the writing of anonymous pamphlets, such as the one on Wycherley,[1] where he scandalously attacked Pope and drew from the satirist that scornful exclamation about 'Gildon's venal quill.' He was associated with John Dunton, the eccentric, unscrupulous bookseller and journalist, and wrote for him the *History of the Athenian Society*, by which Dunton's Athenian Gazette was made to appear, what it was not, the scholarly enterprise of a serious society. In his *Miscellany* and *Chorus Poetarum* he recklessly labelled with the names of Spenser and Milton poems which were certainly not by those authors. It is probable that he was also the author of *The Post Boy Robbed of his Mail*, five hundred letters addressed to 'persons of several qualities,' a

---

[1] It is only fair on Gildon to add that this life of Wycherley is not in existence, and may well have been a pure invention on the part of Pope during his campaign against Addison, who, he asserted, had bribed Gildon with ten guineas to write the pamphlet.

series which repayed him so well that two years later he published a second instalment.

All this does not constitute a very creditable record, and when in 1696 we find Gildon following up the success of Southerne's *Oroonoko* with a collected edition of Mrs Behn's *Histories and Novels*, it is inevitable that we should regard the anonymous *Life and Memoirs* prefixed to that edition with some suspicion. In 1696, her play, *The Younger Brother*, had been posthumously published under Gildon's auspices, preceded by his (signed) *Account of the Life of the incomparable Mrs Behn;* and later in the same year the collected *Histories and Novels of Mrs Behn* were published by Gildon, preceded this time by the *Life and Memoirs* 'written by one of the fair sex.' Now who was this lady? She gives us no hint of her identity beyond saying that she was a gentlewoman of Mrs Behn's acquaintance, who 'knew her intimately well,' and Dr Bernbaum's assumption is, of course, that Gildon wrote the *Life and Memoirs* himself. He may well be right. Gildon, as we know, was an adept at literary hoaxes, and moreover it had already occurred to him in his own avowed *Account* of Mrs Behn that: 'To draw her to the life, one must write like her, that is, with all the softness of her sex and all the fire of ours.' I think it extremely likely that he afterwards amplified his two and a half pages into the larger document, and doubtless relished the piquancy, so much to his own taste, of ascribing the work to a woman.

The authorship of the *Life and Memoirs* is not perhaps a very interesting question; the only really pertinent point is that it should have been written by somebody who had known Mrs Behn, and in either case, whether it was written by Gildon or by a woman, this first-hand knowledge seems to be beyond dispute. Gildon had known her; he came to London in 1686 and she did not die until 1689, which gives him three years of possible acquaintance, quite long enough for a pushing young man and an easy-going woman to ripen that intimacy which he afterwards claimed. The

Life and Memoirs is not a very skilfully compiled record, it lacks proportion and,—especially in the later editions,—contains some absurdly impossible stories, but as a contemporary account one must make the most of it, in default of something better, as a guide to the subsequent events of Aphra's life.

2

THE SURINAM episode over, the Amis family returned to England and took up their residence in London. A little strange, perhaps, after their familiar life with Trefry and Harry Martin and the other members of the small English colony; rather grey, the London skies, after that country where it was eternal spring. But Aphra, according to his biographer, fell at once upon her feet, thanks to her good looks and wits, and it was not long before a Dutch gentleman, a merchant, of the name of Behn, in easy circumstances, pressed his suit and persuaded her to become his wife. 'They are mistaken,' says her biographer, 'who imagine that a Dutchman can't love, for though they are generally more phlegmatic than other men, yet it sometimes does happen that love does penetrate the lump.'

A brief but brilliant stage of her career followed close upon this marriage. She was now a respectably married woman, well-off, in her 'twenties, full of sparkle and liveliness, and in this character she appears at the court of Charles II, where her brilliant youth is said to have attracted the attention of the King. How far this may be true is impossible to determine; gossip readily associated the name of any attractive young woman with that of the King, and nothing is more likely than that her biographer, anxious to paint her in as interesting a light as possible, should have hinted quite unjustifiably at such a thing. Indeed, the hint is so slight that it may well not have been meant as a hint at all. We are told simply that she amused the King by

her wit, and gave him so pleasant and rational an account
of Surinam, and particularly of the misfortunes of Oroonoko,
that he desired her to deliver her experiences publicly to the
world. ' One of the Fair Sex ' definitely says of *Oroonoko*
that it was written by the command of King Charles the
Second. But as Dr Bernbaum justly observes, had the King
really desired her to do this, she would certainly have obeyed
with alacrity, and the world would have had *Oroonoko* in
1666, with a fulsome dedication to his Majesty, instead of
in 1688, with a dedication to Lord Maitland, and not so
much as a passing reference to his Majesty's suggestion. At
the same time, a verse lies obscurely buried in Aphra's
poems which may perhaps refer to this incident of her brief
career at court. It occurs in a Pindaric ' On Desire ':

> Where wert thou, oh malicious sprite,
> When shining Honour did invite?
> When interest called, then thou wert shy,
> Nor to my aid one kind propension brought,
> Nor wouldst inspire one tender thought
> When Princes at my feet did lie.

It is a somewhat ambiguous verse, which may be inter-
preted according to the taste of the reader, and is here offered
without comment.

This period of ease and success, however, was but a flash
in the pan. Aphra's troubles were only about to begin. Her
husband dying in 1665 (was it of the plague?) threw her
impoverished and alone upon the world. Why her husband
did not leave her his fortune, we are not told ; nor are we told
why she did not return to her family in this emergency, but
it may be fair to assume,—knowing what we do of her free
and pleasure-loving nature,—that independence was dearer
to her than domestic comfort. It is also possible, of course,
that her recent exploits, at the Court and elsewhere, were
not of a kind to win the approval of Mrs Amis of Wye.
She may have been beginning, at this time, to feel like the

hen who has hatched a duckling. She must, indeed, always
have had a suspicion that her daughter Aphra was something
out of the common,—that precocious childhood, that scribbling of verses, was not the usual thing in the yeoman families
of Kentish villages, whether they transferred themselves to
tropical colonies or not,—and now here was Aphra marrying
a Dutchman and blossoming out into a wit and beauty at
the Court, not the most exemplary of Courts. What was
to follow? Mrs Amis, having other daughters to think of,
may well have withdrawn; Aphra, tired of the maternal
protection, may well have tossed her head and struck out
for herself; it is all conjecture. At all events it is certain
that it was not to her family that she turned, but to the
Court. The surprising thing is that we should still hear of
Mrs Amis at intervals, coming to her daughter's assistance,
even when that daughter had grown into the detached,
adventurous, soon to become notorious, Mrs Behn, a rôle
in which she persists, with varying fortune, until the end of
her life. The secret service, a debtor's prison, a merry
career as playwright and libertine, fame, friendship, love—
all this was to be hers, but throughout all her vicissitudes
the adventurous, independent character is dominant: she
followed the path that she had chosen. She was never a
prudent woman; her nature was too rich and warm for
that, she who was ' of a generous and open temper, something passionate, very serviceable to her friends.' Scrapes
she might get into, friends might fail her; but always she
emerges gay, energetic, courageous, giving; a lovable
creature, a born Bohemian. Probably Mrs Amis, of Wye,
had a weakness for her troublesome daughter; but she must
herself have been an unusually loyal mother not to sheer off.

3

POOR MRS AMIS. At Surinam she had had Aphra
safely under her eye; returned to London, she had got

Aphra safely and prosperously married; if Aphra went to Court, and made herself conspicuous there, that was surely Mr Behn's business; but now here was Aphra a widow, applying to her friends at Court and getting herself sent to Holland as a spy. Mrs Amis disappears for the moment from the record of Aphra's life. Perhaps she went back to Wye; we are not told. Aphra was on her own; a spy in the English secret service,—English relations with the Dutch being at that time difficult and dangerous, and Aphra's Dutch name no doubt a useful, because disarming, asset. I suggest also, what I have not seen suggested elsewhere, that she may well have been considered to have acquired valuable experience of the Dutch in Surinam. Whatever the reason or reasons for her appointment may have been, Aphra, as an accredited agent, arrived in Antwerp in the summer of 1666, taking with her forty pounds, her entire fortune.

It was not primarily with the object of spying on the Dutch and searching out their naval projects that she was sent abroad. Any information which she could incidentally collect on naval matters would of course be welcome, but her real business there was to keep a watch on such renegade Englishmen as were living in Holland, and seeking, in treasonable alliance with the Dutch, to overthrow the existing English monarchy. She was especially charged with the task of getting into touch with one William Scott, son of a regicide, himself of questionable loyalty in the past, but now, ' though at first shy,' eager to re-establish himself in the favour of the King. Scott had already received a command to return to England, but was evidently unwilling to obey before he should have been granted a free pardon, and this pardon he was prepared to earn by betraying his Dutch friends and collaborating with Mrs Behn as a spy in the English service. About ten days after her arrival she writes home to say that she has seen him, and that he is prepared to co-operate with her if she will consent to live in Holland and not at Antwerp. She has already spent her £40, and asks for supplies. She calls Scott, Celadon, for reasons of discretion; and she to him is Astrea, a name which thus had its origin in political intrigue, but which was later to win its fame in literature. This letter, naturally, was not addressed to the King. It was sent to James Halsall, the King's cupbearer.

Mrs Behn is now deep in political intrigue, though the financial support from home scarcely corresponds to the importance of her mission. Her letters from the very first are plaintive and soon become urgent. On the 27th of August she writes her second letter to Halsall: the place is expensive; she has been reduced to pawning one of her rings; will he send her some money? On the 31st she writes to Halsall again, and on the same day to Tom Killigrew. To Killigrew she unburdens herself: she is obliged to trouble him, for she can get no answer from Halsall. On Scott's account she has had to pay £20; on her own account she owes £25 or £30; she has brought only £40 with her; and meanwhile the necessities of existence are costing her ten guilders a day. £50 is required to clear her of debt. She has written to Halsall, explaining her difficulties, but Halsall refuses to answer. On September 4th she writes again to Killigrew, begging not to be made incapable of serving through want of money; she has pawned all her rings; the place is so dear she has been unable to buy so much as a shoe to travel in; £100 is now needed to pay her debts. Again, no answer. On September 14th she writes to Halsall, a letter full of naval and political news; evidently she wanted to impress him with her efficiency, for there is no mention of money. But things are getting desperate. Three days later, on September 17th, she writes again to Killigrew, complaining much of Halsall's silence which puts an end to all service, and begging again for money. Scott, thanks to his secret meetings with her, has attracted the notice of one Corney, ' an insufferable, scandalous, lying, prating fellow,' who is spreading rumours about Scott's relations with Mrs Behn and has even threatened Scott with

assassination. Aphra says his ' tongue ought to be clipped.'
By September 21st it appears that Scott has had word from
England, for Aphra writes to Halsall that he is overjoyed
with the promise of his pardon, but she herself is ' almost
out of her wits ' at not receiving any answer to her letters,
and begs again that she may be sent some money. Still no
answer.

In all these letters she either sends naval and political
information, or else encloses a long report from Scott, for in
the midst of her distress she was still eager to do her duty.
Her letter to Halsall of September 25th consists entirely of
news.   But in the meantime her position has become
critical, for on November 3rd she writes at last in despair to
Lord Arlington, then Secretary of State. She came over to
Antwerp, she says, on his lordship's business. No one in
the world but herself could have drawn Scott into the service.
She has written constantly to the authorities at home, begging
for encouragement and for supplies, but can get no answer.
She is in debt and in extreme want; she has pawned her rings
and all she had; now she is likely to lose all her remaining
possessions and to be put in prison. All this time she has been
working hard, and has forwarded a mass of information, for
which her only reward is silence and neglect. She begs now
that she may not be ruined and disgraced in a strange place,
and entreats his lordship to help a poor stranger, whose life
and death are in his hands.

Incredible though it seems, this letter also remained un-
answered.   Christmas came; Astrea had now been in
Antwerp for five months. The day after Christmas she
wrote again to Lord Arlington. She applies to him, she
says, as her last hope and the fountain of mercy; did she
not know so well the justice of her cause, she would be
wild with her hard treatment. The delays have caused her
twice the expense she would have had, but she would not
beg or starve, so she has had to get credit. Scott is already
in prison for debt, and if relief is not forthcoming she herself

will speedily follow him there. She desires much to come home, if only she had money; she cannot return without this; she is a poor stranger, and her life depends on it. Will his lordship send her the £100 to settle up her affairs and enable her to return to England? If she cannot take the next convoy, she will have to stay two months longer. She did not,—indeed she did not,—desire the place or the voyage, and her only wish now is to come home.

The appeal could scarcely have been more piteously worded, but it met with no response. Realising that at last she could expect no help from those at home, in whose service she had expended the whole of her meagre fortune, but must rely on her own efforts to extricate herself from her hopeless position, she raises a loan of £150 from one Edward Butler, in England, and finally sails for London in January 1667.

This account of Mrs Behn's brief and disastrous adventure in Antwerp we have from the undisputed testimony of her own letters and Scott's, seventeen in all, which are preserved among the State Papers of the reign of Charles II. But that evil genius of confusion, always at work where Mrs Behn's biography is concerned, puts up its head again and a regular farrago of romance comes to blur the sharp outlines which her letters have, for once, given us. The author of the *Life and Memoirs* is, of course, to blame. There is, first of all, the story that Mrs Behn gave her Government warning of the projected Dutch attack upon the Thames and the Medway, but this story, for historical and chrono-logical reasons into the detail of which I need not enter, may be at once dismissed. Mrs Behn, to put it briefly, could not have known of the Dutch attack, since it was not planned until several months after she had left Antwerp. Secondly, the *Life and Memoirs* relate with a great deal of circumstantial detail, reinforced by letters purporting to have passed between Aphra and her Dutch lovers, a series of politico-amorous intrigues with two rival suitors, one ' a

spark whom we must call by the name of Van der Albert of
Utrecht,' and the other a ' hogen-mogen Nestorian ' called
Van Bruin. Father Summers suggests that this story and the
letters were ' pure fiction,' the sweepings of Aphra's desk,
intended by her to have been worked up into a novel, but
discovered later on by Gildon and included (whether as
bona fide documents or with the intent to mislead) in the
Life and Memoirs. Whether the biographer was honest or
not, there the story stands in print.

The letters are written in Aphra's usual racy style:
' Though our courtiers will not allow me to do any great
matters with my politics, I am sure you must grant that
I have done so with my eyes, when I shall tell you I have
made two Dutchmen in love with me. Dutchmen, do you
mind me, that have no soul for anything but gain; that
have no pleasure or interest but the bottle. . . . Yet I,
sir, this very numerical person your friend and humble servant, have set two of them in a blaze; two of very different
ages. Van der Albert is about thirty-two, of a hale consti-
tution, something more sprightly than the rest of his countrymen. . . . My other is about twice his age, nay, and bulk
too, though Albert be not the most Barbary shape you have
seen; you must know him by the name of Van Bruin. . . .
He had not visited me often before I began to be sensible
of the influence of my eyes on this old piece of worm-eaten
touchwood.' Van Bruin avows his passion in a letter to his
' most transcendant charmer,' and Aphra replies: ' Extraordinary sir, I received your extraordinary epistle, which has
had extraordinary effects, I assure you, and was not read
without an extraordinary pleasure,' all in a gay and frivolous
style, until Van der Albert disposes of Van Bruin, and she
herself disposes of Van der Albert by sending him back to
his wife. Such is the story, amplified by further accounts
of how Mrs Behn's companion, ' an old woman of near
threescore, guilty of the common vice of age, Avarice . . .
was corrupted by Albert's gold to put him dressed in her

night clothes to bed in her place,' and other incidents which
bear, to say the least of it, a suspicious family likeness to the
regular stock-in-trade of Restoration comedy and the Italian
novella. ' Have I now caught thee, thou malicious charmer? '
cries the merchant's son, leaping into Aphra's bed and finding
there, not the old woman, but the disguised Albert.   It is
all good farce, and whether it is true or not does not, after all,
very much matter.

Even concerning so simple a thing as Mrs Behn's return
journey to England, her biographer has left us a fabulous and
inexplicable account.   One begins to believe that there was,
about her personality, something which from the first
attracted the veils of legend.   She could not be allowed to sail
simply from Antwerp to London without meeting on the
Channel that ' strange apparition ' which made Sir Bernard
Gascoigne conclude that painted glasses had been put at the
ends of his Italian telescopes to amuse and surprise those
who looked through them; so he took the glasses out,
rubbed them, and put them in again, but still beheld the
same thing floating towards the ship, so near now as to be
plain to the naked eye.   Aphra was said to assert that the
whole company saw it,—' a four square floor of various
coloured marbles, from which ascended rows of fluted and
twisted pillars, embossed round with climbing vines and
flowers and waving streamers that received an easy motion
from the air; upon the pillars a hundred little Cupids clam-
bered with fluttering wings.'   This surprising phantom,
watched, according to Aphra, by the whole company
gathered together on their deck, ' came almost near enough
for one to step out of the ship into it before it vanished ;
after which, and a short calm, followed by so violent a storm
that having driven the ship upon the coast she split in sight
of land; but the people, by the help of the inhabitants and
boats from the shore, were all saved; and our Astrea arrived
safe though tired to London, from a voyage that gained her
more reputation than profit.'

How did this story find its way into the *Life and Memoirs* ?
Clearly, either Aphra or her biographer was romancing.
Sir Bernard Gascoigne did run into a storm, but his ship was
not wrecked, and extravagant pavilions are not commonly
met with on the English Channel. Then again, why does
the author of the *Life and Memoirs* say that Mrs Behn's
maiden name was Johnson? If the author, Gildon or one
of the fair sex, really knew Aphra ' intimately well,' we
might at least expect that he or she should know so elementary
a detail as the name of the subject of the memoir. That he or
she should have underestimated Aphra's age is understandable,
if we remember that he or she was trying to clear Aphra of
the accusation of having been Oroonoko's mistress. But the
rest must remain a problem.

4

T I R E D, T H E N, but safe, Astrea arrived in London. It
was not the London that she remembered. During her
absence in Antwerp, a month after she had left England,
the Great Fire had in four catastrophic days reduced the
City to an unrecognisable waste of havoc. Wind had spread
the flames, and over an area of more than four hundred
acres, four hundred streets and courts gaped with the ruins
of thirteen thousand houses. Fantastic sights were to be
seen: whole streets of brick chimneys stuck up to heaven,
the houses once around them having disappeared; the steeples
of the City, solitary landmarks, towered above the unidenti-
fiable devastation; you could stand where Cheapside had
been and see the Thames; a crop of wooden shelters clus-
tered among the blackened ruins under the dirty snow.
While Mrs Behn struggled in Antwerp, and met William
Scott in secret, and despatched those urgent letters to Killigrew, London had burned.

In January 1667, when she reached London, no
rebuilding had as yet begun. On January 17th Pepys could

write: ' I observe still in many places, the smoking remains of the late fire'; therefore Mrs Behn, if she wandered beyond Temple Bar, must have observed it too,—wreaths of black smoke creeping up underfoot, from some buried cellar where the coal still smouldered. The cold that winter was exceptionally severe; prices had risen beyond all reason; rents were prohibitive, lodgings almost unobtainable; and moreover, Mrs Behn, although safe in body, was, at the time of her return from Antwerp, financially already on the rocks. She must have passed that year, 1667–1668, in conditions of the most abject misery. Her poor depleted purse, depleted in the interest of an ungrateful and even dishonest Government, was all she had brought back from five months' service in Antwerp; that, and the £150 debt to Edward Butler, which she had no means of cancelling until her arrears of salary should be paid over to her. This treatment of Mrs Behn is a black mark against the names of Lord Arlington and the King. She had laboured conscientiously, she had run certain risks, she had in all things (so far as we know) comported herself as a loyal servant of the Government. We know enough, I think, of her robust and ardent nature to argue that whatever she undertook she would not do by halves; no one who wrote with so vigorous a pen could be lethargic in the affairs of life; and moreover we have her letters to prove that any information she acquired was immediately sent on to England whatever personal difficulties she was experiencing at the time. There can be no excuse for the King or his ministers.

Yet it was not for want of complaints on Aphra's part that her bill remained unpaid, for she complained loud and often. Butler was pressing for his money; if Mrs Behn cannot pay, then she must go to prison. The first petition is mildly worded; evidently, with incorrigible optimism, Aphra still had confidence that the justice of her claims would in the nick of time be recognised. She merely asks the King for an order to Mr May or Mr Chiffinch for pay-

ment of the money due to Mr Butler, she being threatened
with an execution. But as no notice was taken of this, her
tone in the next petition, and especially in the letter annexed
to it, rises to a shriller and more desperate note. Fyhare
[*sic*] Behn petitions his Majesty, to order £150 to be paid
to Edward Butler, who threatens to use all severity with
herself if it is not paid within a week. Mr Halsall and Mr
Killigrew know how justly it is due. The covering letter
to Killigrew makes almost unbearable reading: ' Sir,' she
writes, ' if you could guess at the affliction of my soul, you
would, I am sure, pity me. 'Tis to-morrow that I must
submit myself to a prison, the time being expired, and though
I endeavoured all day yesterday to get a few days more, I
cannot, because they say they see I am dallied withal, and
so they say I shall be for ever, so I cannot revoke my doom.
I have cried myself dead, and could find in my heart to break
through all and get to the King, and never rise till he were
pleased to pay this; but I am sick and weak and unfit for it,
or a prison; I shall go to-morrow. But I will send my
mother to the King with a petition, for I see everybody are
words, and I will not perish in a prison from whence he
swears I shall not stir till the utmost farthing be paid; and
oh God, who considers my misery and charge too, this is
my reward for all my great promises and my endeavours.
Sir, if I have not the money to-night, you must send me something to keep me in prison, for I will not starve. A. BEHN.'

Aphra had now reached the lowest point she was to touch.
No notice was taken of her appeal, Butler carried out his
threat, and she was duly thrown into the debtors' jail. Her
third and last petition was sent out from there: Fyhare
Behn to the King, not to let her suffer for what was done
for his Majesty, but to order the payment of £150 to Edward
Butler, who on Lord Arlington declaring that he had neither
money nor orders about it, threw her into prison.[1] Thus

_____
[1] These petitions are all undated, but are classified in the State Papers
under the year 1668.

Lord Arlington failed her; Killigrew failed her; and,
bewildered, incredulous, outraged, she found herself at last
actually in the place to which she can never have believed
that her misfortunes would lead her.

The prisons must, moreover, at that date have been in
a peculiarly loathsome condition. Every one of the City
prisons had been destroyed or rendered useless by the
Fire, including Ludgate and the Fleet, the traditional
places of incarceration for debtors. It is impossible to
say where Mrs Behn was sent. Perhaps to Newgate,
which was hastily patched up after the Fire; perhaps to
Caronne House, in South Lambeth, which had been acquired
to shelter the homeless rabble of debtors from the Fleet.
Wherever it was, the imagination really recoils at the
thought of the squalor and overcrowding which must have
prevailed, for not only had the usual number of prisoners
to be housed, but that number was enormously increased by
the unfortunate citizens who, having lost all their property
in the Fire, were unable to meet their obligations. So
serious did the problem become that in 1671 an Act of
Parliament was passed for their relief, specially mentioning
those who had suffered by ' the sad and dreadful fire,' but
this Act came too late to be of any use to poor Mrs Behn.
For her, on the contrary, as she lay on her pallet, came
nothing but a swelling stream of destitute refugees, victims
of bankruptcy and of pitiless creditors, herded into quarters
quite inadequate to accommodate them. Where was that
vast rock of white marble? Where were the little waves
still dashing and washing? Where was that country of
eternal spring? Where were Trefry and Oroonoko? Their
place had been taken by those officials of whom she was to
write, with such a sudden burst of bitterness, ' the vermin
of the parish, I mean the overseers of the poor, who eat the
bread from 'em.'

How long she remained in prison is not on record: we
do not even know whether Mrs Amis, gallantly coming to

the help of her disconcerting daughter, carried Aphra's final
petition to the King; all we know is that the debt was at
last paid and that Aphra, showing a fine and magnanimous
spirit, could later write of Killigrew with esteem and admiration (she who could sooner forgive an injury than do one),
instead of lashing him with the contempt he deserved, a
contempt whose vocabulary she had so thoroughly at the
command of her pen.   Thanks at last to some benefactor,
or to the awakened conscience of his Majesty's ministers,
Aphra emerged from the squalor of jail, a free woman, to
enter upon the third and most brilliant stage of her career.

I

MRS BEHN was now approaching thirty, and the moment had arrived when she was to discover her true vocation. She had been a colonist's daughter, she had been a wife, a widow, and a spy, she had known brief prosperity, she had lived through the extremes of poverty and despair, she had seen the inside of a London prison; now she was thrown upon the world of London, with her way to make and the experience of those thirty years behind her. They had taught her something; they had taught her, at last, to arrange her life; they had taught her to take what she wanted. 'The rest of her life was entirely dedicated to Pleasure and Poetry.'

Sensible Astrea. Miss Julia Kavanagh, writing in 1863, thought otherwise. But Astrea, living in 1670, knew that her two great assets were her charm and her pen, and she had no scruples about using both to procure for herself the comfort, fun, and popularity, that she desired. 'Give me but love and wine,' she exclaimed:

'Give me but love and wine, I'll ne'er
Complain my destiny's severe.
Since life bears so uncertain date,
With pleasure we'll attend our fate,
And cheerfully go meet it at the gate.
The brave and witty know no fear or sorrow,
Let us enjoy to-day, we'll die to-morrow.'

The author of the *Life and Memoirs* candidly remarks

that as Mrs Behn was a woman of sense, by consequence
she was a lover of pleasure, 'as indeed all, both men and
women, are.' She never forgot how pleasant it was to be
in love; how many idiots love had made wise, how many
fools eloquent, how many home-bred squires accomplished,
how many cowards brave. She is very tender to her wild
young men: her Rover, after five acts of outrageously
caddish behaviour, is allowed to paint himself in these
engaging colours:

> I wish I were that dull, that constant thing,
> Which thou would'st have, and Nature never meant me.
> I must, like cheerful birds, sing in all groves,
> And perch on every bough.

She prized freedom, and constantly and gaily advocated that
the heart should bestow itself where it listed: ' Marriage is
as certain a bane to love as lending is to friendship; I'll
neither ask nor give a vow,'—it is her perennial refrain.

> The stealths of love, the midnight kind admittance,
> The gloomy bed, the soft breath'd murmuring passion,—
> Ah, who can guess at joys thus snatched by parcels?
> The difficulty makes us always wishing,
> And every blessing seems a kind of rape.

But if she was tender to the rake, how justly does she
deride the fop and man of fashion, the ' beastly town fool,
monstrum horrendum ': in whose company we might pre-
sume much of her time to have been spent, and from whose
pocket much of her income to have been derived. ' Our
Astrea,' says her biographer, ' had many of these [sots and
fools] who professed not a little love for her, and whom she
used as fools should be used, for her sport and the diversion
of her acquaintances. I went to visit her one day, and found
with her a young brisk pert fop very gaily dressed, and who
after an abundance of impertinence left us.' And what
good has she to say of him and his like? No more good than

have any of her contemporaries; she is never tired of be-labouring him. A country fop, indeed, is a tolerable animal, but the town fop is the most unmanageable beast in Nature. He believes that the languishing turn, the toss, and the back-shake of the periwig is the direct way to the heart of the person he adores. He is the plaything of love, the sort of animal with whom love sports but never wounds. His glass is every moment called to counsel, his valet consulted and plagued for a new invention of dress; he spends his morning in the composition of *billets-doux* and madrigals, he carries his hat under his arm and puts his other hand carelessly into his bosom, as if laid upon his heart; his head is bent a little to one side, though not enough to disarrange his cravat or wig, and sometimes the glove is well-managed and the white hand displayed. He is, in fact, a most accom-plished ass; he only talks of love, but thinks himself that happy thing, a lover, and while wanting fine sense enough for the real passion, believes what he feels to be it. But he feels nothing; for this is he, of all human kind, on whom love can work no miracles.

It must have been a bold fop, after that, who dared to ogle Mrs Behn.

2

HOW DANGEROUS, however, are these literary exer-cises! how fatally easy to construct a case, almost any case, by a little adjustment of the data! The temptation is great, and the opportunities are many. It is peculiarly difficult to judge of the convictions of a writer; we are placed, at one and the same time, at an advantage and at a disadvantage: at an advantage, because no one reveals himself so volubly, so unreservedly, or so adequately as a writer; at a disadvan-tage, because we can never be sure when, thanks to some obscure psychological complexity, he is not expressing the precise opposite of what he actually practises and believes.

Thus, though it would be a possible contention that Mrs
Behn's pen wrote, and wrote with gusto, words which
Mrs Behn's tongue would have refused to utter, the con-
verse might equally have chanced to be true.   One function,
and that not the least delicate function, of the commentator
is to discriminate between the passages when his author is
reflecting a genuine conviction, and when he is not.   The
author did not intend to be dishonest, but he was the un-
conscious victim of his own psychology;   the commentator
does not intend to be dishonest, but he is the equally uncon-
scious victim, unless he is very much on his guard, of a
crop of false deductions.   The difficulty is increased when
the author happens to be a playwright, for then many
opinions must be placed in the mouths of characters, who
reflect no personal likeness of their creator.   How then is
the critic to proceed?   Only on the accident of repetition
can he base his deductions ;   that is, when a topic obviously
preoccupied the author, so that it crops up again and again
throughout his work, nagging, haunting, importunate ;   as
in the case of Mrs Behn (a woman, an unconventional
woman, and a woman dependent for her existence upon her
own efforts), the topic of love: love freely given;   love
bought and sold;   the pains and pleasures of love in either
of those manifestations.

I have myself devised at least three theories, all based on
her own writings, to explain Astrea's morals.   All are
equally satisfactory, all equally untrustworthy, and the
truth probably lies, as usual, in a judicious mixture of the
lot.   I believe that she was a woman capable of sincere
passion, capable consequently of suffering through the dis-
appointments and disillusions of such passion, but sometimes
driven (a) by necessity, and (b) by a loose, pleasure-loving
temperament, into more cynical, incidental liaisons of which
she, at heart, disapproved.   This is not a sentimental but
a reasoned conception of Mrs Behn, keeping the traps and
dangers always well in view.   It is based not only upon her

Love-letters, but upon the constant harping in her writings on that theme of love bought or given, simulated or genuine; speeches which may be put into the mouths of her characters, but which none the less allow of no doubt at all as to the side on which her sympathies lay.

> According to the strictest rules of honour,
> Beauty should still be the reward of love,
> Not the vile merchandize of fortune,
> Or the cheap drug of a church-ceremony.
> She's only infamous, who to her bed
> For interest takes some nauseous clown she hates;
> And though a jointure or a vow in public
> Be her price, that makes her but the dearer whore.
> All the desires of mutual love are virtuous . . .

And again:

> Take back your gold, and give me current love,
> The treasure of your heart, not of your purse.

Examples could be given in any quantity. It is because she wrote with so much zest and appreciation of the gay and gallant and luxurious; because she loved everything that was light-hearted, reckless, and extravagant; because she wrote bawdy and no doubt talked bawdy too, and was as careless as she could be about her morals, that her fundamental honesty and idealism have never been sufficiently insisted on. It may seem absurd to apply the words to Aphra Behn. Let it be clearly understood that I am making no attempt to whitewash her, or to represent her as other than she was. She meant to enjoy herself, and she meant to be a popular writer; she was an attractive woman, so she found plenty of men ready to make love to her; her tastes were naturally coarse, the tastes of her day were coarse, so she gratified both herself and her audience by indulging in coarseness: the resultant conception is of a dissolute woman and a porno-graphic author; a conception which is only up to a certain point correct. I think it is easy to prove from her own writings that she retained a very true sense of proportion; that she never lost the faculty of seeing life from the outside; and that her scorn of falsehood was at least as great as her delight in pleasure. In other words, Mrs Behn, properly edited—and quite apart from the *Love-letters to a Gentleman*, which are not to be put into the same category as her professional writings—may be represented as an exceedingly moral and idealistic writer.

Bawdiness was not the thing she really believed in. It amused her and it paid, but it was not the be-all and end-all of existence. Nor was light love the only kind of love, for ' there are in the quiver of the god a great many different darts; some that wound for a day, and others for a year; they are all fine, painted, glittering darts, and show as well as those made of the noblest metal; but the wounds they make reach the desire only, and are cured by possessing, while the short-lived passion betrays the cheat. But 'tis that refined and illustrious passion of the soul, whose aim is virtue and whose end is honour, that has the power of changing nature . . .'

' What a lewd world we live in! Oh London, London, how thou aboundest in iniquity! Thy young men are debauched, thy virgins deflowered, and thy matrons all turned bawds.'

And again, ' how short life was, and how transitory its joys; how soon she would grow weary of vice, and how often change to find real repose in it but never arrive to it.' That is the accent of one who has suffered and learnt to apprise. All her outbursts, that gash the page in the midst of the conventional intrigue, have the accent of experience: ' In that country . . . where the only crime and sin against a woman is to turn her off, to abandon her to want, shame and misery: such ill morals are practised only in *Christian* countries, where they prefer the bare name of religion, and, without virtue or morality, think that sufficient.' There is

a personal bitterness in such writing which breaks through
the flippant phrases. Instead of dwelling so much upon
Astrea's ' trolloping muse,' and of trying to mitigate her
indelicacy by advancing her as the first abolitionist, her
critics would have done better to seek out these chance
flashes of indignation, compassion, and human understand-
ing. Swinburne came near to an estimate of her when he
spoke of her ' instinctive Christianity '—a bold term to
use of one who, with her customary courage and good sense,
had remarked that the introduction of Christianity would
but disturb the tranquillity of the heathen Indians. But
Swinburne was right, as the anonymous biographer was
right who preferred Astrea to all the canting tribe of dis-
semblers that die with the false reputation of saints.

3

W H O ,   T H E N , were her lovers? Her biographer says
that she enjoyed the love of not a few of different characters,
besides the friendship of the most sensible men of the age,
but her own poems are peopled only with Lycidas, Amintas,
Alexis, Lysander, Philaster, seldom giving a clue to their
real names. Consequently, they figure as swains rather than
as men of flesh and blood; Mrs Behn herself, perhaps conscious of this, was careless about the labels under which she
disguised them. John Hoyle, for instance, who usually
appears in her poems as Amintas, turns into Lycidas in *Our
Cabal*. There are contemporary references to her inti-
macies: ' If you give yourself but the trouble of examining
an old poet's[1] conscience . . . I don't question but you'll
there find *Mrs Behn* writ as often in black characters, and
stand as thick in some places, as the names of the generation
of Adam in the first of Genesis,' and so on.

The only man, however, whom we know for certain to
have been her lover was John Hoyle, a lawyer of Gray's Inn

[1] Probably Edward Ravenscroft.

and the Inner Temple, a very disreputable person whose presence among Mrs Behn's intimates may be taken as evidence, if that were needed, of the rakish company she kept. Was she really in love with Hoyle? Was it thanks to Hoyle that she could, on occasion, write so bitterly? Was it owing to Hoyle's parsimony or even to his indigence that she remained so unaccountably poor? Did he, instead of giving her money, help her merely by writing some scenes in her plays? Did she, in return, share her poor earnings with him? Did he repay her passion with indifference? Was Hoyle responsible for the tormented unhappiness in her *Love-letters to a Gentleman?* Very little is known about him. Mrs Behn tells us that he was a wit uncommon and facetious, a great admirer of Lucretius, which is, at any rate, something to his credit. In 1660 he was admitted to Gray's Inn, in 1679 to the Inner Temple. In 1687 he was indicted at the Old Bailey, on a charge of misconduct with a poulterer. In 1692 (but that was after Aphra's death) he was murdered in a tavern brawl by a young Mr Pitts, and in a contemporary commonplace book there is the comment: ' Mr Hoyle was an atheist, a sodomite professed, a corrupter of youth, and a blasphemer of Christ.'

4

IN TOM BROWN'S *Letters of Love and Gallantry* there is a letter from Mrs Behn to Mr Hoyle, ' occasioned by the report of his too close friendship with young F——ws.' Tom Brown, of course, is by no means a reliable authority, and it is quite possible that he composed the letter himself, but as some other letters of Mrs Behn's in the same collection are obviously genuine (notably the one to her friend Mrs Emily Price on the subject of *Abedelazar*), it is equally possible that the one to John Hoyle is genuine too. But if genuine, it must have been written after Mrs Behn's passion for him had died (arguing on the assumption that

John Hoyle was indeed the man who inspired the *Love-letters to a Gentleman*), for although she appeals to him in the name of ' our past endearments,' it is the perfectly calm letter of someone in concern about the welfare of a friend and bears no resemblance to the wild suffering of the *Love-letters*. She was, in fact, at the time of writing, still fond in a friendly way of Hoyle, but not in the least in love with him. ' Oh! clear yourself instantly from these black aspersions, or you'll soon become a jest and by-word to all who know you: you begin already to be the aversion of the fair sex, and will quickly be the scorn of your own too. . . . Let me beg of you, therefore, nay, let me conjure you in the name of friendship and by all our past endearments, to think of some remedy to retrieve your sinking reputation.' And, to point her moral, she encloses by way of postcript the poem which in her collected works is given as *The Disappointment*, but which here is called *An Imperfect Enjoyment*.

How different is the tone of the *Love-letters!* These extraordinary documents, eight in number, are included in the 1696 edition of the collected *Histories and Novels* as a separate section; but in subsequent editions they form part of the introductory *Life and Memoirs*, and are headed by the words: ' Printed from the original letters.' No one, I think, could read them without being convinced of their authenticity. So personal and poignant are they that one reads them almost with a sense of indiscretion; a sense of having forced Astrea's desk and eavesdropped on her during her absence. Quotation can give no real impression of their urgency; of the constant begging that he will come to see her; that he will not break with her altogether; that he will not desert her: they are more the letters of a man to a woman than of a woman to a man. (This was, perhaps, all things considered, inevitable.) But they are convincing not only by their passion, but by their incidental verisimilitude. There is no attempt to compose them into the continuity of a story; they read as letters passing between people

who are in constant touch, as a slice cut out of a prolonged
relationship. They are scattered with all the casual detail
of a day-to-day diary. There are references to days of the
week: will he come on Thursday morning, or, better still,
on Wednesday night? There are references to her ordinary
life: 'Though it be very late, I cannot go to bed, but I must
tell thee I have been very good ever since I saw thee, and
have been a-writing, and have seen no face of man, or other
body, save my own people.' There are references to things
they have done together; thus, after they had obviously
been together at a friend's house, she writes to him when
she has got home: ' I stayed after thee to-night till I had
read a whole act of my new play, and then he (?) led me
all over the way, saying, Gad, you were the man . . . so
he went on awhile and all ended that concerned you. And
this, upon my word, is all.' That is not fiction. That is a
woman scribbling a midnight letter to a lover. The very
style is completely different from even Astrea's literary
style, colloquial though that habitually was.

Astrea was in love, and most unhappily in love. ' You
are so unreasonable,' she writes, ' you would have me pay,
where I have contracted no debt; you would have me give,
and yet, like a miser, would distribute nothing. You would
not be in love for all the world, yet wish I were so. Possibly
you will wonder what compels me to write? what moves
me to send where I find so little welcome; nay, where I
meet with such returns; it may be that I wonder too.
Was that, my friend, was that the esteem you profess?
Who grows cold first? Who is changed? and who the
aggressor? 'Tis I was first in friendship and shall be last in
constancy. Renounce your false friendship, or let me see
you give it entire to   Astrea.'

She had been right to dread losing her heart to him. ' If
you are destined to be he, the Lord have mercy on me, for
I'm sure you'll have none. I was born to ill-luck.' But
for all her apprehensiveness she was fairly caught, though

she still struggled and threatened to shake herself free. ' I
grow desperate fond of you, and would fain be used well; if
not, I will march off. Do not shame me with your perpetual
ill-opinion: my nature is proud and insolent and cannot
bear it.' Her nature, indeed, comes out in the letters with
the absolute ring of truth, generous, passionate, proud, un-
compromising. Reading them, one is overcome with indignation at Hoyle's reluctance as a lover, till one reflects that
perhaps, after all, he could not help himself, and then the
full tragedy of the situation breaks over one with all its
force. Astrea, unsparing, ardent Astrea, born to ill-luck,
had given her heart to the wrong man. At moments she
was even tempted to think that he disliked her: ' How
could anything but the man that hates me entertain me so
unkindly? Witness your excellent opinion of me; witness
your passing by the end of the street where I live, and
squandering away your time at any coffee-house, rather than
allow me what you know in your soul is the greatest blessing
of my life, your dear dull melancholy company.' So, he
liked her,—' witness your excellent opinion of me,'—but
he did not love her; he did not return her passion. He was
openly unfaithful to her; did not spare her feelings; told
her with a brutal candour his reasons for leaving her:
' You left me to torments. You went to love, alone, and
left me love and rage, fevers and calentures, even madness
itself. Indeed, indeed, my soul, I know not to what degree
I love you; let it suffice I do most passionately, and can
have no thought of any other man whilst I have life. No!
Reproach me, defame me, lampoon me, curse me and kill
me when I do. Farewell. I love you more and more
every moment of my life. Know it, and good night.

Astrea.'

5

BUT IF ASTREA'S private life was thus dark and
tormented, her outward life in the light of day was at least

full of incident, excitement, and success. It appears from a passage in Tom Brown's *Letters from the Dead to the Living* that she soon became a figure in London, an Egeria to the younger generation of writers, an acquaintance to be sought, a mistress to be boasted of. ' You were the young poets' Venus; to you they paid their devotion as a goddess; and their first adventure, when they adjourned from the university to the town, was to solicit your favours. . . . Oh! that I had but one glance into your own accounts; there, I am sure, should I find a complete register of all the poets of your standing, from the Laureate down to the White-friars ballad-monger.' But although Mrs Behn was the centre, and no doubt the brilliant centre (for all are agreed as to her wit and her conversational powers), of a clique of admirers, there were others who viewed with resentment the first attempt of a woman to compete as a writer with the men.

Astrea was meeting the professionals on their own ground, she was even crowding them off the boards of the Duke's Theatre. There were only two theatres in London, and if one of them was presenting a play by Mrs Behn it obviously could not be offering its hospitality to a play by anybody else. Mrs Behn herself soon became alive to the conspiracy that was organised against her, and expressed herself with her usual liveliness and vigour on the subject. ' That day 'twas acted first ' (she is referring to her play *The Dutch Lover*), ' there comes me into the pit a long, lither, phleg-matic, white, ill-favoured, wretched fop, an officer in masquerade newly transported with a scarf and feather out of France, a sorry animal that has naught else to shield it from the uttermost contempt of all mankind, but that respect which we afford to rats and toads . . . this thing, I tell ye, opening that which serves it for a mouth, out issued such a noise as this to those that sat about it, that they were to expect a woeful play, God damn him, for it was a woman's.' Of another play (*Sir Patient Fancy*), not produced until 1678,

she was still to write,—for the persecution continued, and
this time the ladies of the town were to take a hand in it,—
'The play had no other misfortune but that of coming out
for a woman's; had it been owned by a man, though the
most dull unthinking rascally scribbler in town, it had been
a most admirable play.   Nor does its loss of fame with the
ladies do it much hurt, though they ought to have had good
nature and justice enough to have attributed all its faults to
the author's unhappiness, who is forced to write for bread
and not ashamed to own it.'   She must have got into the
habit of anticipating trouble, for at the end of *Sir Patient
Fancy* what does she do but bring forward Mrs Gwynn to
look about the house and speak the epilogue:

> There and there o'erheard a coxcomb cry,
> ' Ah, rot it! 'tis a woman's comedy,
> One, who because she lately chanced to please us,
> With her damned stuff will never cease to tease us.'
> What has poor woman done, that she must be
> Debarred from sense and sacred poetry? . . .
> To all the men of wit we will subscribe,
> But for your half-wits, you unthinking tribe,
> We'll let you see, whate'er besides we do,
> How artfully we copy some of you:
> And if you're drawn to th' life, pray tell me then
> Why women should not write as well as men?

But, if she could be effective in self-defence, she could also
be wildly and imprudently unscrupulous.   Imprudently, for
her inaccuracy offered a new handle to her persecutors.
Thus in the preface to the *Lucky Chance*, attacked on the
score of indecency, she lashes out: ' I challenge anyone to
point me out the least expression of what some have made
their discourse; they cry, *That Mr Leigh opens his night-
gown when he comes into the bride-chamber ;* if he do, which
is a jest of his own making, and which I never saw, I hope
he has his clothes on underneath?   And if so, where is the

indecency?' Thus Mrs Behn in the preface, but how does
the scene stand in the printed version of the play? Is her
outraged indignation justifiable? Far from it:

Sir Feeble Fainwould : My gown, quick, quick,—t'other
sleeve, man,—so now my night-cap; well, I'll in, throw
open my gown to fright away the women, and jump into
her arms. (Exit Sir Feeble; next scene changes to the bed-
chamber. Enter Sir Feeble. Throws open his gown, they
[the women] all run away, he locks the door.)

Sir Feeble : So, so, now we're alone, Leticia—off with
this foolish modesty, and night-gown, and slide into my
arms.

Thus, though Astrea was attacked, she knew how to hit
back, even unwisely, being fortunately of a fighting temper
which supported her against ill-luck, enemies, and illness,
and the other odds of a difficult but, on the whole, trium-
phant life.

6

THE YEAR 1670, then, finds Mrs Behn in London, not
famous yet, but marshalling her forces; associated with
aspirant writers, actors, actresses, and rakish tavern characters; about to launch her first play upon the world of Restoration London. Just as she herself was emerging from
disaster, laboriously rising from the lowest rungs of her
fortune, so London was beginning to rise from its embers.
By 1670, when Astrea's first play was launched at the
Duke's Theatre, London instead of cringing in a low
huddle of rubbish had shot up into a high maypole of scaffold-
ings. Debris had been cleared away, and the City Surveyors
had staked out their claims. Those wild flowers which had
sprung out of the crevices of the ruins,—that ' London
Rocket,' which still goes by the popular name,—had been
uprooted, and their wild encroaching loveliness was rapidly

giving place to the return of bricks and mortar. A spirit of
activity and busyness pervaded the city. The plashy slap
of the bricklayer's trowel was everywhere audible, and the
brisk tock-tock of the builder's hammer; so Astrea's pen
scratched over the paper, and the wild flowers of her early
experience gave way before the more substantial edifice of
her fame. Astrea, although born under the green hill at
Wye in Kent, was a true child of London. It was in London
that Astrea, whose destiny had taken her to Surinam and
Antwerp, was to find herself. So it was with the rising of
the new London that *The Forced Marriage, or, The Jealous
Bridegroom* was produced at the Duke's Theatre in Decem-
ber 1670.

In this connection we have a story which well illustrates
Mrs Behn's imprudent but endearing kindness to her friends.
Among her acquaintances at that date was young Thomas
Otway, aged nineteen, an undergraduate of Oxford, burning
to try his luck as an actor; and to him, with a spontaneity
and a rash good-nature typical of her who never learnt
worldly wisdom, she allotted the part of the King. It was
ill-advised, it was no doubt most unpopular with the other
members of the company; but the author would have her way:
Otway was charming, eager, good-looking; if he wanted
his chance, he should have it. The result was disastrous.
' Mr Otway, not being used to the stage, the full house put
him to such a sweat and tremendous agony, that he could not
utter a word of his part.' The scene is related by old
Downes, the prompter and rich London character, one who
from his youth had been ' bred up behind the curtain,' and
who was particularly well qualified to sympathise with the
collapse of the young aspirant, having himself at the beginning of his career suffered a similar humiliation in the
presence of the King, the Duke of York, and a house
crowded with notabilities. Father Summers thus vividly
reconstructs the unfortunate first night: ' The heavy
curtain drew up and showed a conventional scene of a

Palace, and Otway, made up with white hair and white
beard, clad in rich velvet robes and ermine, wearing a
jewelled crown and clasping the golden sceptre in his
hand, was seated on his canopied throne as King of
France with all the court about him. . . . The King
opens the play:

> How shall I now divide my gratitude
> Between a son and one that has obliged me
> Beyond the common duty of a subject?

But Otway with parched throat and trembling limbs found
himself unable to articulate the words.   His glazing eyes
saw as through a mist the candle-lit theatre, tier upon tier
of faces, the fine ladies, brave in silk and satin, sparkling with
gems, that lined the boxes, the gallants leaning over them
to pay compliment and pretty speech which need not be
over-nice or over-delicate, the young blades in the pit
fooling with saucy orange-girls and their dear covey the
sharp-tongued, black-vizored whores.   The sweat poured
down from his forehead.   He well-nigh swooned, and his
failure was complete.'

Where, meanwhile, was Aphra Behn?   Not in the front
of the theatre, surely, where the audience must have rocked
over poor Otway's discomfiture, but at the back somewhere,
peeping anxiously from the wings, or wringing her hands
behind the scenery, as the collapse of the play became more
and more evident.   Did Otway come, still in his white
beard, trailing his velvet robes, and crowned with his tawdry
crown, dithering with shame and stage-fright, to implore her
forgiveness?   That she gave it is evident, for they remained
fast friends, and Otway, when his name was made (though
not as an actor), was loyal enough to defend her against her
critics as she had been generous enough to forgive him for
wrecking that first play on which must have been concentrated all her hopes.

7

N E V E R T H E L E S S , the play was not completely wrecked,
but ran for six nights, which sounds little to our ears, but
which for that day was no contemptible record. By the
time her third play, *The Dutch Lover*, was produced in
1673, Mrs Behn was a recognised figure, a force to be
reckoned with, and the cabal against her had consequently
grown to serious proportions. It was no easy path that she
had chosen to tread. She had not only her jealous opponents
to fight, but the incompetent actors that represented her
characters. The play was hugely injured in the acting, the
negligence of some was intolerable, her Dutch Lover was
a Jack-pudding, who filled out his part with idle stuff of his
own invention, and, for a last misfortune, the person who had
promised her the epilogue failed to keep his word. Small
wonder that *The Dutch Lover* was not a success.

Is it too fanciful to attribute to this disappointment the
three years of silence which follow? Or was she perhaps
resting on her laurels? She might be abused, there might
be a clique determined to destroy her, but at least she was
recognised, at least she had a name that came frequently up
for discussion in the coffee-houses and the drawing-rooms.
She was attacked, but she was not ignored. She was Madam
Behn, she was Astrea, the incomparable, the admired, the
ingenious, the divine, the lovely, the witty, the heroine of a
hundred odes and poems. Side by side with this adulation
ran the current of criticism; she was belittled on several
counts: she allowed her lover to help her with her plays,
she stole plots wholesale, she was lewd. Against all these
accusations she defended herself with spirit; nevertheless
the fact remains that between the production of *The Dutch
Lover* and of *The Town Fop* three years were allowed to
elapse. What was she doing meanwhile? Surely her silence
was not due to lack of invention, for ' her muse was never

subject to the curse of bringing forth with pain, for she always writ with the greatest ease in the world, and that in the midst of company and discourse of other matters,' and considering that only eighteen years of her life were given up to literature she may be reckoned a voluminous writer. After 1676, when she re-entered the arena with the *Town Fop*, she produced plays and novels every year. *The Debauchee, The Counterfeit Bridegroom, The Rover, Abdelazar, Sir Patient Fancy, The Young King, The Feigned Courtezans, The Roundheads, The City Heiress, The False Count*, all followed each other in quick succession from 1676 to 1682. After 1682 Mrs Behn temporarily abandoned the theatre, and probably the reason is not far to seek. In August of that year a tragedy called *Romulus and Hersilia, or The Sabine War*, was produced at the Duke's Theatre. The play was anonymous, but the prologue and epilogue were written by Mrs Behn, who by two previous plays had offended the susceptibilities of the Whigs, living at that time in a ferment of political dissatisfaction, and eager for revenge against the lampoons of the Tory playwrights. The prologue and epilogue to *Romulus and Hersilia* furnishing her enemies with sufficient pretext, a warrant was issued against ' Mrs Aphaw Behn ' for committing several misdemeanours and making abusive reflections upon persons of quality, and for having written scandalous speeches without license or approbation of those that ought to peruse and authorise the same. It was therefore required that Mrs Aphaw Behn should be taken into custody and brought up to answer for the said offence.

There is no record that the threat was carried out, but Mrs Behn had had her fright, and her next appearance in print is made with a prose work, the *Love-letters between a Nobleman and his Sister*, and in the following year with the collection of her poems, nor did she return to the stage for five years. *The Love-letters* were very popular, but it is evident from a letter written by her at this date that despite their success she was again in financial difficulties. It looks almost as though she were supporting John Hoyle instead of being supported by him. Existence was indeed precarious for ' Astrea with her soft gay sighing swains,' her success, her swelling reputation, her enemies literary and political, her kind-heartedness, her generosity, her independence, and her defiance.

' Dear Mr Tonson,—As for the verses of mine, I should really have thought 'em worth thirty pound, and I hope you will find it worth £25. Not that I should dispute at any other time for £5 where I am so obliged, but you cannot think what a pretty thing the Island will be, and what a deal of labour I shall have yet with it; and if that pleases, I will do the second Voyage, which will compose a little book as big as a novel by itself. But pray speak to your brother to advance the price to one £5 more, 'twill at this time be more than given me, and I vow I would not ask it if I did not really believe it worth more. Alas, I would not lose my time in such low gettings, but only since I am about it I am resolved to go through with it though I should give it. I pray, go about it as soon as you please, for I shall finish as fast as you go on. . . . I wish I had more time, I would add something to the verses. I have a mind to, but, good, dear Mr Tonson, let it be £5 more, for I may safely swear I have lost the getting of £50 by it, though that's nothing to you, or my satisfaction and humour; but I have been without getting so long that I am just on the point of breaking, especial since a body has no credit at the Playhouse for money as we used to have, fifty or sixty deep, or more; I want extremely, or I would not urge this.

Yours, A. B.

Send me an answer to-day.'

How can we explain this? Urgent and ungrammatical, her letter was composed under stress. She had, by that time, produced thirteen plays, most of them successful; she had published the famous and popular *Love-letters between a Nobleman and his Sister*; she had the manuscript of two novels lying idle in her desk; she enjoyed the friendship of men such as Dryden, Otway, and Creech; she had the admiration (which should have been, financially, more to the point) of half the sparks and wits in London: why then should she 'want extremely'? Either she was inordinately extravagant or less cynically mercenary than has commonly been supposed. Consider, too, the undertaking which she gives in the following year (1685): 'Whereas I am indebted to Mr Baggs the sum of six pound for the payment of which Mr Tonson has obliged himself. Now I do here empower Mr Zachary Baggs, in case the said debt is not fully discharged before Michaelmas next, to stop what money he shall hereafter have in his hands of mine, upon the playing my first play till this aforesaid debt of six pound be discharged.'

A miserable sum, but Zachary Baggs must be satisfied. As for Mrs Behn, if she could not be sure of finding six pounds between the 1st of August and Michaelmas she must indeed have been in sad straits. We may deduce that Mrs Amy Amis, that staunch and long-suffering mother, was also in low water,—if indeed, she was still alive—else surely she would have come to the rescue. Astrea's poverty seems incomprehensible, unless we are to conclude that she was a hopeless spendthrift, an assumption which would be perfectly in keeping with all that we know of her nature. These rare letters, these occasional indications rising to the surface, bubbling up out of the past, are inadequate guides to the reconstruction of an entire existence, with its busyness, its population, its movement, its comings and goings, its jollity and its despondencies.

8

I N 1686 Mrs Behn took to the stage once more with *The Lucky Chance*, one of her best comedies. Its indecency, however, brought more abuse showering on her head, and again she flew out at her persecutors. Again she protested that had the play been written by a man, it would have been well received, though it is criminal because a woman's. 'This one thing I will venture to say, though against my nature, because it has a vanity in it: that had the plays I have writ come forth under any man's name, and never known to have been mine, I appeal to all unbiassed judges of sense, if they had not said that person had made as many good comedies, as any one man that has writ in our age; but a devil on't the woman damns the poet.' She was incensed, she was hurt. Even her friends were not always loyal to her: 'I cannot omit to tell you that a wit of the town, a friend of mine at Wills' Coffee-house, the first night of the play, cried it down as much as in him lay, who before had read it and assured me he never saw a prettier comedy. . . . All I ask, is the privilege for my masculine part, the poet in me. . . . If I must not, because of my sex, have this freedom, I lay down my quill and you shall hear no more of me, no, not so much as to make comparisons, because I will be kinder to my brothers of the pen than they have been to a defenceless woman, for I am not content to write for a third day only.[1] I value fame as much as if I had been born a hero; and if you rob me of that I can retire from the ungrateful world and scorn its fickle favours.'

Needless to say, the indomitable Astrea neither laid down her quill nor retired from the world, but produced instead, in the following year (1687), a farce (*The Emperor of the Moon*), a translation of Fontenelle's *History of Oracles*, a translation of Æsop's Fables, and four novels. Nevertheless, the words just quoted give a fair idea of her state of mind. She had struggled, she had been beaten down and had risen

---

[1] The whole profit of the third day's performance went to the author. 'There's nothing makes them [the poets] so thorough-stitched an enemy as a full third day. That's crime enough to load it with all manner of infamy.'

up again, she had befriended others, she had been laughter-
loving and warm-hearted, she had known good moments
and bad, and through all she had carried her spirit unbroken.
One could wish that she might have been left to enjoy in
peace the success that her courage deserved. But now in the
middle 'forties she must add another enemy to the phalanx.
She had never been strong, and now she writes of herself as
' ruffled, and ill-natured grown with pain.' A new picture
of her appears in the lampoons; she is no longer the brilliant
Astrea, exasperating because successful, a butt for envious
abuse which after all was a form of compliment; she has
become an old and ill woman:

> Long with a sciatica she's beside lame,
> Her limbs distortured, nerves shrunk up with pain,
> And therefore I'll all sharp reflections shun:
> Poverty, poetry, pox, are plagues enough for one.

This cruel verse, with its terrible last line, paints altogether
too painful a picture of the merry Aphra in the last two years
of her life. Writing to Waller's daughter-in-law, she ' can
only say I am very ill and have been dying this twelve-
month,' and in a pathetic postscript apologises for the illegi-
bility of her letter: ' I humbly beg pardon for my ill-
writing, Madam, for 'tis with a lame hand scarce able to hold
a pen.' Even now that lame hand still laboured. In her
last eighteen months her output was considerable: another
translation of Fontenelle, some poems, a metrical version in
English of Cowley's *Trees*, and five novels, *The Fair Jilt*,
Agnes de Castro, *The Lucky Mistake*, *The History of the Nun*,
and *Oroonoko* itself. This is surely an extraordinary record
for a dying woman, shattered by constant pain. In March,
only a month before her death, she was publishing the
Pindaric in which she thanks Dr Burnet for his benevolent
enquiries after her, and declines the suggestion which he
had evidently made, that she should celebrate the accession
of William of Orange. It would seem, from the text of

the poem, that she had suffered in some way from the change
of monarch, for she writes:

> Though I the wondrous change deplore
> That makes me useless and forlorn,
> Yet I the great design adore,
> Though ruined in the universal turn.
> Nor can my indigence and lost repose
> Those meagre Furies that surround me close,
> Convert my sense and reason . . .

If this be so, it was fortunate for Mrs Behn that her life
was not to be prolonged into a reign which would have
regarded her with disfavour. On the 16th of April, 1689,
at the age of forty-eight, she died, and—final and most
astonishing contradiction—she who for the immorality of
her life and the indecency of her writing had been so severely
censored by all the prudes of the town, was buried in Westminster Abbey, under an epitaph said to have been composed
by John Hoyle:

> Here lies a proof that wit can never be
> Defence enough against mortality.

9

IN POVERTY and pain the chequered life of the famed
Astrea had worn itself to an end, crowned at the last by
that inexplicable honour, but the echoes of her celebrity
and of the rancour that it had evoked were to rumble on
for some years after her death. Her manuscripts were in
the hands of her friends, Gildon and one G.J.[1]; there were
unpublished novels and unacted plays; there was scope for
a collected edition of her works, and for a biography of the
author; there was a chance of money to be made, and Gildon

[1] George Jenkins?

had always been obliged to live by his wits. Besides, he may
have been genuinely fond of Mrs Behn and honestly anxious
to do the best he could by her memory. But both Gildon
and G.J., in their rôle of impresario, had many difficulties
to contend with, difficulties which they were by no means
successful in surmounting. They meant well; they secured
the services of no less a person than Dryden himself, to
usher in the first play with a prologue; but the party against
them was too strong. That faction which had persecuted
Astrea living was not inclined to spare Astrea dead. *The
Widow Ranter*, an excellent play, produced under G.J.'s
auspices in 1690 at Drury Lane, was damned from the first,
as ' the best play that ever was writ must prove so, if it have
the fate to be murdered like this,' by the mangling that it
underwent and the lamentable casting and acting of the various
parts.

So perverse was the choice of actors, indeed, that it seems
as though the management of Drury Lane, inspired by the
enemies of the dead author, was determined to ruin poor
Astrea even as she lay in her grave. For instance, the part
of Daring, a young and attractive officer with whom the
Widow Ranter is in love, was given to Samuel Sanford, an
actor usually reserved by the company to play the part of
such twisted villains as Iago, ' for his figure, which was
diminutive and mean (being round-shouldered, meagre-
faced, spindle-shanked, splay-footed, with a sour countenance
and long lean arms), rendered him a proper person to dis-
charge Iago and Malignii in *The Villain*.' This is Anthony
Aston's description of him, and Cibber calls him ' an excellent
actor in disagreeable characters,' which was ludicrously the
reverse of what Mrs Behn had intended for her handsome
Daring. Whimsey, Whiff, and Boozer were equally badly
cast, and their excellent comic parts cruelly truncated. G.J.
was full of a loyal indignation; he dedicated the play to a
Madam Welldon, knowing that Mrs Behn in her lifetime
designed to dedicate some of her works to that lady, and

wrote: 'Our author, madam, who was so true a judge of
wit, was (no doubt of it,) satisfied in the patroness she had
pitched upon: if ever she had occasion for a wit and sense
like yours, 'tis now, to defend this (one of the last of her
works,) from the malice of her enemies and the ill-nature of
her critics, who have had ingratitude enough not to consider the obligations they had to her when living; but to
do those gentlemen justice, 'tis not altogether to be imputed
to their criticism, that the play had not that success which
it deserved and was expected by her friends: the main fault
ought to lie on those who had the management of it. Had
our author been alive she would have committed it to the
flames rather than have suffered it to be acted with such
omissions as was made, and on which the whole foundation
of the play depended. . . . This play, madam, being left
in my hands by the author to introduce to the public, I
thought myself obliged to say thus much in its defence. . . .'

The *Younger Brother*, produced thanks to Gildon six
years later, fared little better. Yet this time the venture
was well acted and well staged, and Gildon could find no
such excuse for the critics as G.J., with considerable fair-
mindedness, had found. If *The Younger Brother* failed, it
failed because Mrs Behn's enemies were resolved that it
should do so. The play was, in fact, hooted off the stage.
Gildon had done his best. He had altered some scenes, but
his alterations, far from doing damage, were probably an
improvement; he had written, or had caused to be written
' by an unknown hand,' a prologue in which Astrea's cause
was eloquently pleaded. Evidently it had been with some
apprehension that Astrea's friends had decided to try the
luck of the play, and Gildon had spared no pains to propitiate
the audience:

Oh! then be kind to a poor orphan-play,
Whose parent while she lived obliged you all.
You praised her living, and you mourned her fall.

Who could, like her, our softer passions move,
The life of humour, and the soul of love?
For poor Astrea's infant we implore,
Let it then live, though she is now no more.

Whatever Astrea in her pride might have thought of such
piteous cajolery,—defiance being more in accord with her
temper,—at least she could not have complained that her
literary executors were not doing their utmost for her.
But the orphan was not allowed to live. Gildon pretended
an aggrieved surprise: ' Mrs Behn was a woman so accom-
plished, and of so established a fame among the men of sense,
that I could not suppose a very severe treatment from the
town . . . especially when, besides the reputation of the
author, the play itself had an intrinsic merit. . . . So that
I may reasonably impute its miscarriage to some faction
that was made against it, which indeed was very evident on
the first day, and more on the endeavours employed, to render
the profits of the third so small as could be.' Gildon and
G.J. were disgusted. Astrea's two posthumous plays had
been complete failures.

But in 1696 came Southerne's tragedy of *Oroonoko* with
its astonishing success, and Gildon raised up his head. Two
years previously Southerne had achieved success with his
The Fatal Marriage, founded on another novel of Mrs
Behn's, *The Nun, or, the Perjured Beauty ;* this time the
success was even greater, and the fact that the popular
tragedy was called by the same title as Mrs Behn's novel
helped to keep her memory green in the mind of the public.
This was Gildon's chance, and he took it. Following close
on his edition of *The Younger Brother*, with his prefatory
note, came the collected *Histories and Novels* with those
pages of *Life and Memoirs, by One of the Fair Sex*, which
have occasioned so much confusion and controversy. The
pendulum henceforward ceased its violent swinging. Mrs
Behn settled down into an accepted if minor position among

the Restoration writers; her plays were revived at intervals; her novels at intervals went into new editions; her poems were included in various miscellanies; and her name appeared as a matter of course in works relating to the writers of her time.   She ceased to arouse either an exaggerated partisan-ship or a jealous hostility; she took her place finally among those effigies of literature, known to all, and read by none. As the flesh dwindled from her bones and she became a skeleton,—as those who had known her, or who knew others that had known her, died gradually off,—so she ceased to be a woman and shrank to a name.   Fashions changed, and those who had read her with amusement in their youth found her intolerable in their old age.   Still the name endured, queer, outlandish, singular—perhaps her most valuable, though most adventitious, passport to immortality.   Mention her to-day, and some voice will murmur, ' Aphra Behn— ah yes—Love in fantastic triumph sat,—' or with uncon-scious irony, ' A thousand martyrs I have made . . .'

I THE NOVELIST

SOME CONCLUDING estimate of Mrs Behn's work now becomes inevitable. In the foregoing pages, her work has been kept subordinate to her life and to her personality, yet neither life nor personality can be of much interest save in relation to her accomplishment. That she went to Surinam, and cut a figure as a wit in London, is very well, but what has she left behind her that is of any real value? That she opened the way for women as writers, is her principal claim on our gratitude, but still we ask what quality besides courage entitles her to a place in English literature? And instead of extolling her gifts in the management of the comedy of intrigue, we shall do much better to avow frankly that Mrs Behn, given her natural talent, prodigally wasted her opportunities.

For the pity is that Mrs Behn, as a novelist, thought her London experiences beneath the dignity of her pen. She had been granted that gift of God, a free, rapid, and colloquial style, and she neglected to turn it to its best advantage. She trifled with French and Spanish authors, she who might have had honest speech with her countrymen. Of what use to us are these Isabellas, Belvideeras, Rinaldos, and Gonzagos? They get into cupboards, they mistake one another's identity, they are shipwrecked in infancy, they fall in love with their sisters, but not one gleam of interest do they arouse. Ah, Mrs Behn, Mrs Behn! was it for nothing that you were cast into prison? made Grub Street welcome?

knew old Downes and Mr Tonson? Was it for nothing
that you hurried in and out of the green-rooms, bestowing
here a word of advice and there a smile of encouragement?
saw dear Tom Betterton, with his great stomach and short
arms, rehearsing, and Mrs Barry without her make-up,
striving to keep her crooked mouth straight? Oddly enough,
all Mrs Behn's critics have referred to her as a forerunner of
Defoe, which is what she ought to have been and just failed to
be. Was it owing to some unanalysed intuition in the minds
of the critics? or owing perhaps to some vague association
between Oroonoko and Man Friday? Whichever it is, the
critics are very nearly, but just not quite, right. We might
have had the mother of Moll Flanders, and all we get is the
bastard of Mademoiselle de Scudéry.

Stay, though: not quite all. The *Unfortunate Happy Lady*
and the *Black Lady* are just enough to show us what we have
missed. This is London, and rich, seventeenth-century
humour. Mrs Behn could do it when she wanted. The
pity is, that she wanted so seldom, and thought it more
aristocratic to mince through Castille, than to bawl in Alsatia
and loiter arms akimbo through Newgate and Covent
Garden. That loose, expressive style of hers is wholly un-
suitable to the romance of cloak-and-sword. It is not, as she
imagined, cosmopolitan, daring, fashionable; it is simply
the coster-girl dressed up as a lady. There, again, Swinburne
with a stroke of intuitive perspicacity was right (for it is not
to be assumed that he had given very special thought to
Aphra Behn), when he calls her the 'plebeian poetess,' and
speaks of her abused and wasted genius. For it was of the
people that she should have written; of paupers huddled
together on the debtors' bench, of link-boys, of landladies
and ancient pandars. Then indeed, given her vigour and
rapidity, her shameless candour and her knock-about experience, we should have had an earlier Defoe; we should have
had a great realistic painter, own sister to Teniers and
Hogarth; we should have had

The young, the old, the witty, and the wise,
The fair, the ugly, lavish, and precise,
Cowards and braves, the modest and the loud
Promiscuously blended in the crowd.

Mrs Behn, however, would not trust to her own native genius. The most original contribution made by her to English literature was certainly *Oroonoko*, but even in that story, drawn out of her own life, she allowed her readings of the heroic romances to colour her description of colonial existence and to flavour her interpretation of her hero with an air of classic chivalry. Oroonoko resembles those seventeenth-century paintings of negroes in plumes and satins, rather than an actual slave on a practical plantation. She dresses him, it is true, in a suit of brown hollands; but none the less the plumes continue to wave in the breeze and the satins to glisten in the sun. She could not wholly escape from *Le Grand Cyrus*. And naturally, she was in far worse case when she frankly adopted the French, Spanish, or Italian convention; her novels then descend to an intolerable artificiality, and are readable only thanks to their brevity and to the colloquial raciness which was never absent from her style. The brevity of the novels is much to be thankful for. The English novel at that period was undergoing a change; the story, popular in Elizabethan times in the form of the Italian novella, but smothered during the first half of the seventeenth century under the voluminous featherbed of the ' heroic romance,' was now (even as the drama) blossoming for the second time. From the year 1670 onwards, there is an enormous crop of short stories, or longshort stories, scarcely to be called novels, but more properly novelettes, the natural reaction of a flippant and pleasure-loving age. ' Novels are of a more familiar nature [than romances] ' wrote Congreve, himself trying his hand at the new genre in his *Incognita, or Love and Duty Reconciled :* ' Come near to us, and represent to us intrigues in practice,

delight us with accidents and odd events, but not such as
are wholly unusual or unprecedented, such which not being
so distant from our belief bring also the pleasure nearer us.
Romances give more of wonder, novels more delight.' The
French and Spanish tradition of cloak and sword and intrigue is dominant. Criss-cross love, duels, stolen encounters,
abductions, escaped nuns,—such was the paraphernalia of
which these stories were made, and Mrs Behn adopted it
wholesale.

The result is dishearteningly sterile. The English genius
was not created for such artificialities; it seldom wears
fetters with becoming grace. Something ruder and more
barbarous is always trying to burst through. The Elizabethans by the miracle of a young and violent poetry twisted
their Italian borrowings to a dark magnificence of their
own, but their power had not descended to the hand of the
Carolines. The Carolines still borrowed from abroad, but
their transmutations produced no extravagant splendour
such as Webster and Tourneur had produced; they turned,
for one thing, more willingly to the gallant and amorous
than to the tragic and sublime, an affectation of Latin
frivolity which did not sit well upon them. The Goth was
trying to frisk. The Elizabethans, in spite of their Spanish
cloaks and Genoese palaces and sonorous diction, were
speaking in the English language of things which they were
well fitted to interpret: of ambition and adventure, of terror,
superstition, passion, and death. The ' plot ' was but the
excuse for all their turbulence of poetry. The minor
dramatists of the Restoration, Mrs Behn among them, fell
between two stools. With the one hand they clung to the
heroic tradition, while with the other they reached out
instinctively towards a naturalness of speech and manner
which their foreign reading still taught them to mistrust.
Thus in the case of Mrs Behn, as of all those who lacked
the genius of a Congreve or a Wycherley, we get the absurd
spectacle of a right instinct struggling with the affectation

of what was thought to be culture. These flames and charms,
cruelties and languishments, with which Mrs Behn's pages
are besprinkled, are not English speech. Her pen races; it
writes good home-made English; then she recollects herself:
this will never do, we must have some foreign spice to lighten
this English bread. Let us be elegant at all costs. The
cloaked figure in the sombrero is the only ghost which haunts
the Caroline imagination.

The habit of borrowing, then, remained long after the
power of naturalization had gone, and long after the glow of
that fiery poetry had faded. It was perhaps inevitable that
such a furnace should temporarily burn itself out. But
there was that other side of the English genius to which Mrs
Behn might have turned in her novels: the plain, broad,
humorous, English realism that would so excellently have
suited her temper. How briskly she begins, when she writes
of the things she knows, and how all London rises out of
her phrases: ' About the beginning of last June, as near as
I can remember, Bellamora came to town from Hampshire,
and was obliged to lodge the first night at the same inn where
the stage-coach set up. The next day she took coach for
Covent Garden . . .' Here, it is no matter that the heroine
is called Bellamora; she might much more appropriately
have been called Lucy, but that her birthplace is Hampshire
and that she is a stranger in London we never question.
Or take the history of Philadelphia, an innocent and inconvenient sister placed by an unscrupulous brother in a brothel:
' You won't stay late, Mr Gracelove? said the mother of
mischief. No, no, replied he, I will only show the lady a
play and return to supper. What is played to-night? asked
the old one. *The Cheats*, mother, *The Cheats*, answered
Gracelove. Ha ! said Beldam laughing, a very pretty
comedy indeed. Ay, if well played, returned he. At these
words they went down, where a coach was waiting . . . '
It lives, as the lovers on or under balconies can never live.
It lives sufficiently to exasperate us into imagining what

Mrs Behn could have made out of her London had she realised the unexploited treasure that lay at the command of her pen.

2   THE PLAYWRIGHT

A N D   A S   S H E squandered her chances as a novelist,— neglecting to become, as she might have become, an invaluable *genre* painter,—as a playwright, though she did a trifle better, the improvement is so small that it serves only to fill us again with regret. Just from time to time, in her comedies, comes a scene or a character full of good plebeian life. She has been praised for her skill in the conduct of complicated intrigue: a fig for that. There are little thumbnail sketches in the plays of Aphra Behn that are worth all the Hispano-French intrigues in the world. One must wade through tedious pages to reach them; but there they are: short, living, different. Mrs Clacket, Betty Flauntit, a Nurse, a Landlady,—these are English characters in the broad ribald tradition of Juliet's nurse or the wives of Windsor. Take Mrs Grimes, the landlady in *The Lucky Chance, or, an Alderman's Bargain* ; she was Mrs Behn's landlady, or John Hoyle's; in any case, a landlady that Aphra knew:

Gayman. Dear landlady . . .

Landlady. Dear me no dears, sir, but let me have my money,—eight weeks' rent last Friday; besides taverns, ale-houses, chandlers, laundresses' scores, and ready money out of my purse; you know it, sir.

Gayman. Ah, but your husband don't; speak softly.

Landlady. My husband! what, do you think to fright me with my husband? I'd have you to know I'm an honest woman, and care not *this* for my husband. Is this all the thanks I have for my kindness, for patching, borrowing, and shifting for you? 'Twas but last week I pawned my best petticoat, as I hope to wear it again; it cost me six-and-twenty shillings besides making; then this morning my new

Norwich mantua followed, and two 'postle spoons. I had
the whole dozen when you came first, but they dropped and
dropped, till I had only Judas left for my husband.

Gayman. Hear me, good landlady.

Landlady. Then I've passed my word at the George
Tavern, for forty shillings for you, ten shillings at my neigh-
bour Squabs for ale, besides seven shillings to Mother Suds
for washing; and do you fob me off with my husband?

Gayman. Is't come to this, can I not be heard?

Landlady. No, sir, you had good clothes when you came
first but they dwindled daily, till they dwindled to this old
campaign, with tanned coloured lining, once red, but now
all colours of the rainbow, a cloak to skulk in a-nights, and
a pair of —— shammy breeches. Nay, your very badge of
manhood's gone too.

Gayman. How, landlady! Nay then, i' faith, no wonder
you rail so.

Landlady. Your silver sword, I mean—transmogrified
to this two-handed basket hilt,—this old Sir Guy of Warwick,
—which will sell for nothing but old iron. In fine, I'll have
my money, sir, or, i' faith, Alsatia shall not shelter you.

But Astrea's heart is always with her penniless young
rake,—with the Wildings and the Rovers and the Gay-
mans;—she could not resist a wheedling young man, even
when he was of her own creation; and in the end the landlady relents:

'Well,—you have no money in your pocket now, I'll
warrant you,—here,—here's ten shillings for you old
Gregory knows not of. (*Opens a great greasy purse.*)'

Of the same family are Wilding and Mrs Clacket. What
is Wilding?

> He speaks and looks, and loves, like any god.
> All fine and gay, all manly, and all sweet;
> And when he swears he loves, you would swear too
> That all his oaths were true.

Mrs Clacket, however, occasionally loses patience with him:

' By my nose, Mr Wilding! I defy you: I'd have you to know, I scorn any good thing should go by my nose in an uncivil way. Have I been the confidant to all your secrets this three years, in sickness and in health, for richer for poorer; concealed the nature of your wicked diseases under the honest name of surfeits; called your filthy surgeons, Mr Doctor, to keep up your reputation; civilly received your t'other-end-of-the-town young relations at all hours; been up with you and down with you early and late, by night and by day; let you in at all hours, drunk and sober, single and double; and civilly withdrawn, and modestly shut the door after me? '

Unfortunately these passages are few, and very, very far between. Yet it cannot be denied that *The City Heiress*, *The Rover*, *The Feigned Courtezans*, and *The Dutch Lover* are good comedy, and would be quite sufficiently amusing to put on the stage to-day, but that their indelicacy forbids. Mrs Behn, within her limitations, knew how to make a play; so far as she went, she knew her business thoroughly; she could mix her ingredients well, even if she lacked the initiative to depart from the current receipt. She had thought about the making of plays; she had thought coolly, though not with any startling originality, and scattered throughout the Prefaces and Epistles which introduce or defend the plays are evidences that she was potentially a just and rational critic. Her observations are what we should expect from her: always sensible; for about the practice of her own craft she preserved as sound a sense of proportion as she displayed in other matters. ' I think a play the best divertisement that wise men have; but I do also think them nothing so who do discourse as formally about the rules of it, as if 'twere the grand affair of human life.' A good artist, she would have nothing to do with the suggestion that litera-ture might be used as a medium for the amending of men's

morals, 'sure I am no play was ever writ with that design
. . . for plays were certainly intended for the exercising of
men's passions, not their understandings.' This being her
opinion of plays, she studied only to make them as enter-
taining as she could, but: 'indeed, had I hung a sign of the
Immortality of the Soul, of the Mystery of Godliness, or of
Ecclesiastical Policy, and then had treated you with Indis-
cerpibility and Essential Spissitude (words, which though I
am no competent judge of, for want of languages, yet I
fancy strongly ought to mean just nothing,) I were there
indeed sufficiently in fault, but having inscribed Comedy on
the beginning of my book, you may guess pretty near what
penny worths you are like to have, and ware your money
and your time accordingly.' She was aware also of the
tyranny of fashion:

> We are forbid all grateful themes.
> The fulsome jingle of the times
> Is all we are allowed to understand or hear,

but this being so, why then did she not make an effort to
break away from it? The answer may be, that she had
her living to earn, and preferred the safety of the established convention to the dangers of novelty. Or, a
simpler and more comprehensive explanation, she was a
thoroughly competent but by no means a great or creative
writer.

To say—as has too often been said—that she was not creative because she borrowed the plots and even the detail of
her plays, is of course sheer nonsense. Greater writers than
Mrs Behn have borrowed, but no one on that account has
denied them the gift of creation in its highest form. Her
range of interest was, however, extremely narrow; in fact,
there was to her only one really 'grateful theme,' and that
was the theme of sex, in which she does at her best display
a certain shrewd knowledge of human nature. Further

than this, in the creation of character, she cannot be said to
go. It is all very superficial. A few astute observations, of
a rather vulgar kind; a supply of quick and easy dialogue;
and that much-vaunted management of situation: this
constitutes her little stock-in-trade. She shared with many
of her contemporaries the peculiarly Caroline faculty of
marrying the romantic to the everyday; thus in a situation
of the wildest romantic artificiality, her puppets continue to
chatter in the plain (sometimes the very plain) English of
the pot-house and parlour. But still she catches herself up,
still she thinks that she ought to adopt not only the plot
but also the idiom of her model, still she thinks it necessary
to adhere to certain prescribed rules; it is as though she had
used up all her store of initiative and daring in persisting
that she, a woman, might claim equal rights with the men,
and had no reserve left for any further effort. Her defiance
of the conventions consisted mainly in trying to compete
with—I will not say outdo, for I think the indecency of
Mrs Behn's plays has been exaggerated into a sort of
bugaboo,—the men at their own game. The result, is that
her plays, although skilful and lively, present no real interest;
they neither enrich our store of literary acquaintances with
any three-dimensional character, nor reflect any facet of
Mrs Behn's personal sensibility. It is only when a Flauntit
or a Clacket or a Grimes passes briefly across the stage that
our interest stirs, and we wake again to the wholesome sense
of irritation at the waste of opportunity and aptitude.

3   THE POET

MUCH HAS BEEN written about Mrs Behn as a playwright, and as a novelist she has been mentioned from time
to time, but as a poet she has scarcely been mentioned at all.
' Love in fantastic triumph sate,'—how many people can
quote beyond that first splendid line? Yet she herself
claimed that poetry was her talent, so it seems fair to examine,

now that she is no longer there to speak for herself, what justification she had for that arrogance. I cannot help having some respect for the opinion that writers hold of themselves, even though their judgment almost invariably prove to be wrong. Had she said song-writer, we should be all agreement. Her songs were as good as the age allowed them to be; she was no genius to stride out beyond the conventions of her age, but as she was a perfectly competent maker of plays, so was she a perfectly competent maker of the sort of song then in fashion, and occasionally she rose above it, and produced something that was less a song than a pure lyric:

> Love in fantastic triumph sate,
>   Whilst bleeding hearts around him flowed,
> For whom fresh pains he did create
>   And strange tyrannic power he showed:
> From thy bright eyes he took his fires,
>   Which round about in sport he hurled,
> But t'was from mine he took desires
>   Enough t'undo the amorous world.
>
> From me he took his sighs and tears,
>   From thee his pride and cruelty;
> From me his languishments and fears,
>   And every killing dart from thee.
> Thus thou and I the god have armed
>   And set him up a deity;
> But my poor heart alone is harmed,
>   Whilst thine the victor is, and free.

Yes, she could certainly write a song. She could write *The Libertine*:

> A thousand martyrs I have made,
>   All sacrificed to my desire,

A thousand beauties have betrayed,
　　That languish in resistless fire.
The untamed heart to hand I brought,
And fixed the wild and wandering thought.

I never vowed nor sighed in vain,
　　But both, though false, were well received;
The fair are pleased to give us pain.
　　And what they wish is soon believed.
And though I talked of wounds and smart,
Love's pleasures only touched my heart.

Alone the glory and the spoil
　　I always laughing bore away;
The triumphs without pain or toil,
　　Without the hell the heaven of joy.
And while I thus at random rove
Despise the fools that whine for love.

She could write *The Willing Mistress* and *When Jemmy
first began to love*. But all these exercises, excellent as they
are in their own way, rather recall the severe words of
Hazlitt: ' It should appear, in tracing the history of our
literature, that poetry had . . . in general declined, by suc-
cessive gradations, from the poetry of imagination in the time
of Elizabeth, to the poetry of fancy in the time of Charles I,
and again from the poetry of fancy to that of wit, as in the
reign of Charles II.' Astrea set great store by wit, and most
of her poems are neat enough in consequence. Many of
them are incorporated in the plays, where little more than
a light and pleasant refrain was needed. It may seem surprising that she never took to satire; but then, although
often indignant, she was never spiteful. There was no real
vinegar in her mockery.

So her songs, let us concede, are graceful enough; pointed,
gallant. But still we come back to her claim that she was a

poet. The writer of *Love in Fantastic Triumph* was certainly a poet; what more can we bring, beyond the songs,
to support her claim? what sudden accent, from the swell
of her turgid Pindarics?

> So have I seen an unfixt star
>   Outshine the rest of all the numerous train,
> As bright as that which guides the marinei,
> Dart swiftly from its darkened sphere
>   And ne'er shall sight the world again.

Is that poetry? Is this:

> By the sad purling of some rivulet
>   O'er which the bending yew and willow grow,
> That scarce the glimmerings of the day permit
>   To view the melancholy banks below,
> Where dwells no noise but what the murmurs make,
> When the unwilling stream the shade forsakes?

It is very seldom that her voice speaks with even this
hint of the accent of poetry. The songs are, on the whole,
the best that can be claimed for her, and it may be said that
the claim is a modest one. Indeed, this whole estimate of
Astrea's work is perhaps slightly ungracious: it is more in
the nature of reproach than of praise. We concede that she
did certain things well, and then immediately attack her for
not having done different things better,—much as we criticise
Proust to-day for not having concentrated more on the
passions of the human heart, and less on certain worldly as-
pirations with which we are temperamentally unsuited to
sympathise. We grow impatient with the gifts that she un-
doubtedly had, and abuse her for not having exploited other
gifts which would have created for us something more to
our taste. She is an example, we conclude, of those writers
who perversely mistake their vocation. So be it. In the
course of these three months spent in her company, it is

Aphra the woman of whom I have grown fond, to the extent of forgiving Aphra the writer the tedious hours she has compelled me to spend over her volumes. She has puzzled and annoyed me; but it is, in the end, with considerable affection that I record her courage and adversities. Gay, tragic, generous, smutty, rich of nature and big of heart, propping her elbows on the tavern table, cracking her jokes, penning those midnight letters to her sad lover by the light of a tallow dip,—this is the Aphra of whom one cannot take leave without respect.

WHAT WAS the date of Mrs Behn's visit to Surinam? We have a number of conflicting statements to consider. First we have the statement that she went to Surinam as a child. (If she had gone in 1650, the date when Lord Willoughby was first appointed governor of Barbadoes, she would have been ten years old.) Then we have the statement, in *Oroonoko*, that her father died at sea and that his family did not intend to stay long in the place. This is confirmed by the author of the *Life and Memoirs*, who says they only waited for ' the next ships to convey them back to England,' and further insists that Aphra's relations with Oroonoko must have been perfectly innocent, since she was little more than a child at the time. But there is no doubt at all that Aphra is writing of herself throughout as an adult, nor can we ignore various allusions in *Oroonoko* itself, and in the *Life and Memoirs*, which serve to place the action of the story in the years 1665–1666. Aphra says, ' Immediately after his (Oroonoko's) time the Dutch took the colony,' i.e. in March 1667. She refers to the deputy-governor as Byam, and the lieutenant-governor from 1662 to 1667 was in fact one William Byam. She says also that the Lord Governor (Lord Willoughby) was ' every day expected '; now, he had been in the colony from 1664 to May 1665; therefore if Aphra was in Surinam during his absence it must have been after that date, May 1665; and the author of the *Life and Memoirs* makes a reference to ' the Lord, her father's friend, that was not then arrived, perished in a hurricane,' and Lord Willoughby was in fact lost at sea in 1666. It is clear, therefore, that Aphra was not a child at the period of which she writes, but a young woman of twenty-four or twenty-five, in spite of several statements to the contrary.

But if these dates, 1665–1666, are to be accepted, a new difficulty presents itself. We know that by the summer of 1666, Mrs Behn was on secret service in Antwerp, having by that time been not only married, but widowed. She must, therefore, have returned from Surinam, and become successively a wife, a widow, and a spy, in the space of a few brief months. It is possible, of course; it is just possible to squeeze it all in ; but it is not probable.

What is the explanation? I confess that I can find none, save the rather lame evasion that Aphra, in saying that ' immediately after his time the Dutch took the colony,' was guilty of an inaccuracy, and that the author of the *Life and Memoirs* was guilty of similar inaccuracies. This amounts to saying that all the chronological hints furnished by Mrs Behn in *Oroonoko*, and by her biographer in the *Life and Memoirs*, are vague and slovenly, and therefore to be disregarded,—not a very satisfactory explanation, but the only possible one. There are two references in contemporary correspondence which incline me to think that Aphra did not remain in Surinam as late as 1665 or even 1664. One occurs in a letter from Sir Robert Harley's steward on his plantations in Surinam; it is dated January 27th 1663, and contains the phrase, ' The ladies that are here live at St John's Hill.' There is no mention of the ladies' names, and I offer the quotation for what it is worth. Then, on July 27th 1664, one William Gwilt writes to his father in England, informing him that he is on Sir Robert Harley's plantation at St John's Hill, ' with only one negro for a companion.' The ladies, therefore, had gone; those ladies who may have been Mrs Amy Amis, her daughter Aphra, and her other daughter.

Finally, in support of my conclusion that the Amis family returned to England earlier than 1664, I quote the following passage from James Rodway's *Chronological History of the*

Discovery and Settlement of Guiana 1493–1668, [George-town, Demerara, 1888]:

' Lord Willoughby, having been released from the Tower with permission to proceed to Surinam, deputed a relation of his named Johnson as governor of that colony and also to look after his lord's interests in the West Indies. Taking with him his wife and children, and also an adopted daughter named Afra or Aphra Johnson, he sailed for Surinam towards the end of this [here in the margin is written 1658] or the beginning of the following year. He did not, however, live to reach his government, but fell sick and died on the voyage. His widow and the children proceeded to Surinam, where they remained for two or three years, living on one of Lord Willoughby's plantations [but St John's Hill belonged to Sir Robert Harley, not to Lord Willoughby], which was under the management of Mr Trefry, who acted as estate attorney for the lord proprietor.'

Here the date 1658 is clearly given, followed by the re-mark that the family remained in Surinam for two or three years. In passing, I would draw attention also to the curious suggestion that Aphra was an adopted child. I am not at all satisfied in my own mind that the problem of her birth and parentage has been really solved. The persistence of the name Johnson, to my mind, has not been really ex-plained away, even by the evidence of the parish register at Wye.

THE WORKS OF APHRA BEHN

PLAYS   *Produced*

The Forc'd Marriage, or, the Jealous Bridegroom.

Dec. 1670

The Amorous Prince, or, the Curious Husband. Spring 1671

The Dutch Lover   February 1673

The Town Fop, or, Sir Timothy Tawdrey   September 1676

The Debauchee, or, the Credulous Cuckold
    (commonly attributed to Mrs Behn)   1677

The Counterfeit Bridegroom, or, the Defeated Widow
    (commonly attributed to Mrs Behn)   1677

The Rover, or, the Banished Cavaliers.   Part I

Summer 1677

Abdelazar, or, the Moor's Revenge   Autumn 1677

Sir Patient Fancy   January 1678

The Young King, or, the Mistake   Spring 1679

The Feigned Courtezans, or, a Night's Intrigue   1679

The Rover, or, the Banished Cavaliers.   Part II   1681

The Roundheads, or, the Good Old Cause

1681, or Jan. 1682

The City Heiress, or, Sir Timothy Treat-all   1682

The False Count, or, a New Way to Play an Old Game

October 1682

PLAYS   *Produced*

The Lucky Chance, or, an Alderman's Bargain   1686
The Emperor of the Moon   1687
*The Widow Ranter, or, the History of Bacon in
    Virginia*   1690 [posthumous]
The Younger Brother, or, the Amorous Jilt
                                           1696 [posthumous]

NOVELS

The Adventure of the Black Lady, written about 1683–4,
    but not published until 1696
The Court of the King of Bantam, written about 1683–4,
    but not published until 1696
The Nun, or, the Perjur'd Beauty, written (?) but not pub-
    lished till 1697

                                                        Published

The Unfortunate Bride, or, the Blind Lady a Beauty   1687
The Dumb Virgin, or, the Force of Imagination   1687
The Wandering Beauty   1687
The History of the Nun, or, the Fair Vow-Breaker   1688
The Lucky Mistake   1688
Agnes de Castro, or, the Force of Generous Blood   1688
*The Fair Jilt, or, the Amours of Prince Tarquin and
    Miranda*   1688
Oroonoko, or, the Royal Slave   1688
The Unhappy Mistake, or, the Impious Vow Punished
The Unfortunate Happy Lady : a True History, written
    before 1685

MISCELLANEOUS   *Published*
Love-letters to a Gentleman   1696
Love-letters between a Nobleman and his Sister
    (commonly attributed to Mrs Behn)   1684

MISCELLANEOUS *Published*

La Montre, or, the Lover's Watch (prose and verse)   1686

The Case for the Watch (prose and verse)

*The Lady's Looking-glass, to dress herself by, or, the
    Art of Charming* (prose and verse)

Lycidus, or, the Lover in Fashion (prose and verse)

Translation of Æsop's Fables   1687

*Translation from Fontenelle's version of Van Dale's De
    Oraculis Ethnicorum, as the History of Oracles
    and the Cheats of the Pagan Priests*   1687

Translation of Cowley's Sex Libri Plantorum   1689

*Translation of Fontenelle's Theory of the System of
    Several New Inhabited Worlds*   1688

Poems upon several occasions appeared in 1684

SELECT BIBLIOGRAPHY

The Life and Memoirs of Mrs Behn, written by One of the Fair Sex, prefixed to the Histories and Novels, 1696.

An Account of the Life of the Incomparable Mrs Behn, by Charles Gildon, prefixed to *The Younger Brother*, 1696.

The Works of Aphra Behn, 6 vols., 1915, edited by the Rev Montague Summers, with a memoir.

Mrs Behn's Biography a Fiction, by Ernest Bernbaum. Kittredge Anniversary papers, 1913.

Mrs Behn's Oroonoko, by Ernest Bernbaum. Kittredge Anniversary papers, 1913.

English Women of Letters, by Julia Kavanagh, 1863.

The English Novel till 1749, by Charlotte Morgan.

The Short Story in English, by H. S. Canby.

The Cambridge History of English Literature, Vol. VIII.

Calendar of State Papers of Charles II, 1666–1668.

An Impartial Description of Surinam, by George Warren, 1667.

De West-Indische Gids, October 1919: Een Koninklijke slaav in Suriname.

Idem, February 1921: Nog eens: Aphra Behn.

Idem, February 1927: Is Aphra Behn in Suriname geweest? (Three articles by Dr H. D. Benjamins.)

Date Due

OCT 17 1973		
FEB 5 1975		
DEC 15 1999		
FEB 05 1998		
APR 23 1998		
JAN 09 2001		
MAY 16 2003		